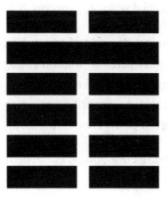

First edition published 2011

Published by The Foundation for Transpersonal Consciousness

© Ná Áak Paola Ambrosi 2011

British Library Cataloguing in Publication Data

A catalogue record of this book is available from the British library

ISBN-978-0-9568403-0-1

The Foundation for Transpersonal Consciousness

AWAKENING
CONSCIOUSNESS

Beyond
2012

Ná Áak
Paola Ambrosi

with contribution from
Stanislav Grof, M.D., Ph.D.

The Foundation for Transpersonal Consciousness

Index

Acknowledgements

You need two to Tango,
Marcus, thank you for the dance

To Malena for piloting the airplane,
To Jorge for keeping us balanced in the air,
To Carlos for helping us to land,
To my mum and my dad for giving us
an airplane to fly!

May we understand the power of our actions
and our inactions,
May we learn to be at peace within,
So the surrounding Universe can become
an experience of peace,
May the dreams be dreamt by the Heart
that breathes compassion,
May we learn to be still and embrace bliss.

To the Great Spirit
That is man,
That is woman,
To the Great Spirit that breathes Life,
To the Great Spirit that breathes Death,
I express my gratitude and awe.

To those whose voices have been silenced or forgotten,
May their song be sung by those who have a voice today and
May we be wise enough not to silence or forget them again,
May we Wake Up!

Ná Áak

A note from the Editor

Awakening Consciousness is a stunning and provocative examination of the human condition from Paola Ambrosi – an author whose deep insights and uncompromising observations challenge the reader to sit up, take notice, take responsibility and, ultimately, take action to respond to the staggering issues we are experiencing on a personal, societal and global basis.

Ambrosi skillfully guides us through the complex intersections of indigenous wisdom, mythology, theology, psychology and other traditions or approaches that try to make sense of our human experience, eventually bringing us to the inevitable and powerful conclusion that there is only one, central truth underlying all of these disciplines and that everything in our experience is delicately balanced and interconnected.

She begins by looking at the 'illness' in our society, uncovering layers of dysfunction and 'ignorance' in and around us with examples and parables. She then explains and clarifies consciousness and unconsciousness; and describes the different 'realities' or mentalities among us. Having established the core issues, Ambrosi attributes the suffering to our fundamental loss of sovereignty. The next chapters lead us through a searing indictment of the systems that have robbed us of that sovereignty – religious, socio-political-economic, health and science.

Finally, Ambrosi draws on the wisdom of the ages, ancient mythology, and current proven phenomena to reveal the essence of the truth of our experience – the realm of Pure Being. The book ends with the answer, the way, the only solution – surprising in its simplicity, but demanding in its practice.

This is a work to be read and re-read; parts of it may need to be absorbed instead of fully understood. It is intelligent, relentless, uncomfortable, and will compel the reader to look at everything in a different light. It's "tough love" indeed, but perhaps that's exactly what we need now. Perhaps we can bear to look at our own 'ignorance' and passiveness; perhaps we can extend our minds to make links and 'join the dots' in a way we never have before. And perhaps some of us will be able to change our lives and the lives of those around us, sending positive ripples out to gradually create a new experience, to awaken a new consciousness.

Paula Reilly

Introduction

*"I belong to no religion,
I belong to no economy,
I belong to no country,
I belong to no society,
Though, I belong.*

*I belong right here,
I belong right now,
I belong outside time."*
Ná Áak

This book is an invitation to the human race to observe deeply what we have become; meditate on the possible reasons that lead us to become what we are today as the inhabitants of planet Earth; and to do something about where we choose to go in the future.

Whenever I used to find myself confused and with no clarity, one of my teachers, kindly and strongly, would remind me about my ignorance with a powerful analogy. This is what he would say to me: "Paola, why do you keep trying the impossible? You are confused and worried; therefore, you have become a storm. When you have been caught in the middle of a storm, you can only wait for it to calm down before you can do anything. But instead, although the storm is blowing with vengeance in your confused state, you are trying to knit a scarf in the middle of it! Think about it! Water is pouring on your face; strong wind is blowing in every direction, blowing your wool away and what is left is all wet and heavy and so are your needles. You can hardly see because the clouds that brought the storm are dark and low. But you, Paola, in the middle of all that, you are trying to knit a scarf!" What used to upset me most was not the ridiculously obvious ignorance I was displaying, but his genuine surprise, which he showed with a patient smile on his face.

As I used to meditate on this teaching, one day a memory became lucid and vivid in my mind. It was the image of a play I saw some time back, and a monologue recreating the life of Einstein. I clearly remembered the theatre; it was the 'Teatro Helénico' in Avenida Revolución, in Mexico City. I remembered I was wearing my mother's jacket because I wanted to look good for my date and I remembered my excitement about the date. At the play I was completely taken into the amazing world of Einstein's mind. In the role of Einstein, Patricio Castillo, a Mexican actor, made a huge impression on me. I was totally absorbed by the inner struggle that Patricio displayed as he embodied Einstein; not being able to engage in an ordinary routine of life because he lived immersed in another reality from where he was downloading information at the speed of light, making it difficult for the world to comprehend what he was talking about.

Patricio showed Einstein's internal devastation when he realised that his discoveries could be used to harm people. He never intended any harm; he cared about evolution not destruction and he could not understand why a government could possible want to use such an amazing discovery of science as a weapon to kill. As these images played in my mind suddenly the internal movie froze and the stage Einstein looked directly at me, pointing his finger, and said: *"No problem can be solved from the same level of consciousness that created it."* He kept repeating this over and over and at this stage I was not sure if my 'memory' was talking directly to me if I was seeing part of the theatre play; or if Einstein was really speaking to me based on what I had read about him. All I knew in that moment was that something deep and wise had been said and I held on to it, knowing it was meaningful because my mind could make sense of it, but not fully understanding it. I held on to it because at some level it resonated in my heart and also because if it had come from Einstein I assumed it was smart, as he was one of my many heroes. As I allowed my meditation to continue, I could not stop the echo of those words in my mind, in my body and in my heart. Suddenly the words stopped being words and became letters; and the letters became sounds, and at that moment my whole being resonated with the experience of what had been said. Although my mind no longer understood it, instead my whole being knew it:

"No problem can be solved from the same level of consciousness that created it"

"Paola, why do you keep trying the impossible?, ...Although the storm is blowing with vengeance in your confused state, you are trying to knit a scarf in the middle of it! Think about it!..."

It then became clear to me that I was trying to solve my ignorant decision to engage in a dysfunctional situation. I was using the same attitude and consciousness that created the problem to try to solve the problem. How could I 'knit' a solution in the middle of the storm that I had created? In that moment, slowly and naturally, all the pieces of the puzzle, teachings I received throughout the years, became one full picture. I had to calm the storm of who I was, the storm of my attachment and fear.

To calm the storm, I had to cease my confusion by ceasing my mind. Clarity would then come naturally as the winds of my mind were calm, and only then would I be ready to knit a solution.

The only way to cease my confusion was to first acknowledge that I was confused and preoccupied because I was living in fear and had attached to fear. Then I had to understand that it was my ignorance that made me confused in the first place. I also had to find a way to detach from my fear and confusion. Finally I had to ensure that I would remain detached from fear and confusion.

Once I had those four steps mastered to a certain extent, I was able to entertain the idea of knitting. The storm had ceased and no more storms were being created. At that stage I had changed the 'mind' that created the problem and I had a different 'mind' or state from which I could knit the solution to the problem.

As long as I remained in the storm I could never find any real and lasting solution. I realised that I had lived in the illusion that the storm was a storm outside myself, completely separate from me and I was powerless to its effects. But I learned that this storm was not outside myself, the storm was *'me'*.

My *stormy* self was responsible for disturbing my surroundings. In the moment I chose to cease my storm I could then see the real *'me'*. It was only then, when I could perceive there were other storms separate from me, I could choose consciously whether to engage with them or to let them pass. Eventually, when a storm would come in my direction, I was calm enough to remain rooted in solid ground and not be blown away by it. At times I learned to surf the winds of the storm when needed, always coming back to the calm waters of my true self.

If we keep trying to figure out how to eradicate the storms of violence, war, recession, depression, psychosis, cancer, AIDS, corruption, etc. we will go round in circles, dispersing ourselves from storm to storm. Until we change the mind-set that created these situations in the first place and made them a storm, nothing will really change.

These circumstances are simply the effects of our collective actions and inactions. They did not appear from thin air. They were created and are fed everyday by us: by you and by me when we forget; when we forget that it is our own inner storm that feeds the hurricane's strength and speed.

We have gotten used to blaming wars, violence, illness, etc., on the government, unstable people, our neighbours, our parents, always someone else outside of ourselves, never acknowledging that it was us who created those things and it is we who are keeping them alive and breathing. Each one of us has contributed to the collective illusion we are living today in society because of our ignorance.

We have to evolve to a place where we can acknowledge that what is *'out-there'* is a reflection of what is *'in-here'*. Until we take that step, we will be like the dog that chases its tail, wondering, debating, having meetings and forums to eradicate what cannot be eradicated, because its cause does not reside in the outside world but in the inside world, in the inside world of who we are.

The question is: are we willing to transform the consciousness that created the disharmony? Are we willing to accept our own individual responsibility in the cosmic dance of the Earth?

Contrary to what the western mind-set informs us, the only way out of the storm we created is through the storm. There is no quick fix or drug that can chase away the illness of ignorance. There are many drugs and legal substances that do a great job in numbing ignorance and the symptoms of the ignorance, but even if we cannot see our ignorance it's still there.

One of the great poets and philosophers of our time, John Moriarty (a man I always admired for his cosmic vision) shares with us in his book *Nigh Journey to Buddh Gaia*:

> "*The drama's done.*
> *The drama of the lobotomizing sword has yielded ground to the drama of the karmic digging fork.*
> *The drama of the lobotomizing sword and bloody sacrifice has yielded ground to the drama of the karmic digging fork and the Tenebrae harrow.*
> *As we might have expected, it was at the heart of the old drama that the new drama had its inception: opening before us and leading us into and through our further and final evolution is*
> *The Triduum Sacrum Trail.*
> *What we yet need to do is to give that trail both architectural and ritual figuration.*
> *Lacking a native shape, we human beings have need of ritual that will give us both shape and direction.*
> *Not that this ritual will be a kind of exoskeleton to us, confining us to fixity of essence and action.*
> *As its name suggests, it is above all else a trail, an implication being that where we once talked about soul as substance we now talk about the adventure of our immortality, and where we once talked about pioneering in ships we now talk about pioneering in prayer.*"
> (John Moriarty)

Can we give up the drama?
Can we give up the 'lobotomizing sword'?
Can we allow ourselves to be lead into and through our further and final evolution?
Can we give the Triduum Sacrum Trail architectural figuration?
Can we give the Triduum Sacrum Trail ritual figuration?
Can we humans create ritual that gives us shape and direction?
Can we humans create ritual that does not confine us to fixity of essence and action?
Can we embark on the adventure of our immortality?
Can we pioneer in prayer?

A necessary step that humanity, as a collective body and as an individual body, needs to take in order to journey, as John Moriarty invites us in his book, into the 'Triduum Sacrum Trail' is to understand that the blood baths, the illnesses and the chaos of society are part of who we are as a human race, as a collective body, as 'We'.

If we continue choosing to stay absorbed in the **'I AM'** and **'YOU ARE'** world: I am a good person, I am italian, I am a factory worker, I am jewish, I am the victim, I am joy, and you are a bad person, you are american, you are a famous star, you are nazi, you are the abuser, you are depressed,... I am you are, I am you are, I am you are, I am you are, I am you are, I am you are, I am you are,...

...I AM RIGHT AND YOU ARE WRONG!

Life will continue to be a place of **RIGHT**: the good people, the saviours, the peace-makers, the nice ones VS the **WRONG** the terrorists, the sinners, the evil, the dark.

Implied in the judgement of **'RIGHT VS WRONG' is WAR** written all over it. This judgement stands in two extreme opposite sides that are in disagreement with each other and therefore allows the **RIGHT** ones to eliminate, murder, blow up, medicate, imprison, discriminate and erase **WRONG** from the face of the Earth.

The next question I have for you is: who is **RIGHT** and who is **WRONG**?

Of course I know YOU are **RIGHT**, so who is **WRONG**? Is it your mother, your father, your son, your daughter, your boss, your teacher, muslims, catholics, jews, democrats, liberals, fascists, capitalists, irish, english, americans, chinese, black, yellow, white, blue, purple, orange, red,...?

It all depends on who answers the question. Doesn't it?

So who will rise above all of these differences and tell us for definite who is **RIGHT** and who is **WRONG**?:

UN?

NATO?

NASA, ESA, CNSA, RFSA?

WHO, FDA, APA?

IMF, WBG, IBRD, IFC, EBRD?

HINDUS, CATHOLICS, BUDDHISTS, JEWS, MUSLIMS, CHRISTIANS?

SETI?

AJE, BBC, CNN, CBS, CCTV?

NASDAQ, TSE, HKEX, DOW?

¥, €, £, $, ?...

These are not random letters to fill space but all organisations, institutions and 'stock' formed by human beings just like you and me deciding the rules, values and importance of the handbooks and manuals of right and wrong doing, good and bad, more valuable or less valuable, healthy and not healthy, all from the level of consciousness:

I AM RIGHT AND YOU ARE WRONG

The only difference is that the decisions are made on a wider scale. At the 'Top' the arguments are not about the dress you are wearing, or the car you drive, or the colour or length of your hair, or if you are christian or mormon. At the 'Top' level the arguments are about:

Do we invade the country?
Do we disclose extraterrestrial life to the public?
Do we ban a plant because it is affecting sales?
Do we introduce arms in the country to provoke civil wars?
Do we steal resources from X because we are running low?
Do we release a pandemic and its vaccination?
Do we shoot the president?
Do we shoot that singer?
Do we shoot that radical?
Do we give a country money and debt?
Do we radiate and inject hormones into food?
Do we create only one currency?

Basically, the implications of the decisions at this level eventually boil down to:

> *"...who will live and who will die..."*
> (Leonard Cohen)

Although a lot of the decisions do not involve a machine gun or a weapon of mass destruction, they do affect individual lives creating ill health, distress and disharmony in society leading to the alienation of what the West calls 'minorities'. We, the people from planet Earth, have been under the foot of 'big empires' that we once called Rome, Spain, United Kingdom, etc. and are now dominated by the empires of World Bank Group, International Monetary Fund, World Health Organization, North Atlantic Treaty Organization, Food and Drug Administration, etc.

The times we are living in are times of change and transformation. Evolution has speed up. The wheel of life has gained momentum and a leap of faith is needed for the wheel to move to a space that can contain its power. All that is happening is that we are jumping a step in the wheel of universal flow. It's nothing new. This has been happening from the beginning of time and will continue to happen eternally.

But right now we are living here and now, witnessing that leap. This is the core message of all of the prophecies and stories about 2012. Yes, there is a cosmic alignment happening, but it is because our galaxy is doing what is has been doing since it was born and before we existed, it is spinning. This natural movement of the universe is giving us the gift to witness evolution. It is a privilege and it should be a time of tremendous joy to stand in the front line of transformation. We are here because at some level we chose to be here. Let's make the adventure worth living by engaging actively and consciously with evolution and life. Let's surf the wind of the storm of life and enjoy the ride.

What this book offers is reflection, prayer and an actualised map of the human being. This encourages us to search for an upgrade in our internal and external computer program. In order to reboot our hard drive and upgrade the programme we need to introduce new algorithms to the software that is currently operating in us as individuals and as a collective breathing body of inhabitants of planet Earth.

The new algorithm is the new Myth of humanity. We cannot run the machine of the human being with outdated algorithms, so as we don't wear the same clothes as our great- great- great grandparents. The clothes are gone because naturally they served their time. They were beautiful and appropriate in the past, but time passed on and they had to change. Now imagine running the computer processor of 2011 with an algorithm (myth) 2000 years old? How can that processor engage in life in the 21st century when it is following instructions that were set in the 1st century? This same argument applies to those alive in 2032, 2052, 2072, 2092, 2112, etc. They will have to actualise and update their programs and the algorithms embedded in order to fully process life at that future time.

If we choose to continue trying the impossible, trying to process today with a computer programme that is incomplete and outdated, then I see little chance of humanity crossing over to the other side of this evolutionary leap. But if we apply common sense, what will happen is not a big apocalyptic scene, although it might look like it, but what we will simply see are computer processors being melted down by the speed and intensity of the new information. Our psyche and physical bodies simply will not have the capacity to compute the change, and in terror of change the circuits will burn down and die.

We are already seeing the effects of this in the outbreaks of suicide, depression, mental imbalance, illnesses such as cancer, or the violence and unrest in countries as the economic systems collapse; the panic and fear as religious institutions are revealed to be corrupt on the inside.

For years we have been running with old programmes that mostly are infected by the virus of fear, attachment and ignorance, which makes them faulty in their nature.

The system needs a cleanup and an upgrade. And what will help us upgrade is to install a new collective and individual myth in our machines. The myth of humanity is its life purpose, the magic that helps humans remember who they are and where they come from. To write a new myth it is essential that we reconcile the split from the different fields of life and within them. We need spiritual leaders to learn about science; doctors to learn about farming; engineers to learn about psychology; politicians to learn about mathematics; lawyers to learn about biology. We need to make it our business to become informed, applying Ervin Lazlo's term from his book Science and the Akashic Field, we have to become:

IN–FORMED

We need to access the *in-formation* of the holographic universe in order to have an updated version of our computer programme. This does not mean that everyone should become the same. On the contrary, it means to embrace the full potential of who you are as a unique and perfect individual as much as who you are in the bigger picture of the story of the inhabitants of Planet Earth.

It means to retrieve our sovereignty, to become the highest power, to become independent thinking individuals as opposed to puppets of WHO, FDA, NATO, NASA, IMF, etc.

It's interesting to see that the two areas showing the biggest cracks and most flaws (running with outdated programs-myths-algorithm) are Spirituality/Religion and Psychology.

Our Spirit and our Psyche.

The very essence of who we are. I see this as a result of having lost our sovereignty in the moment we became afraid and forgot who we were. We are divided in many religious churches, each one of them stating that they have the one absolute truth and that anyone on the outside is condemned or out of grace. On the other hand, Psychology is split into countless schools of thought and approaches, all in conflict with each other, again acting out the paradigm of 'I am right and you are wrong'. In this spiritual and psychological warfare we can see the turmoil that the majority of the world is experiencing within themselves; the struggle to find meaning, to finding a 'god' to believe in. The struggle to understand if we are our thoughts, dreams, memories, unconscious, experiences, or our behaviour and actions. What determines who we are? How can we reconcile our internal split, the split of our minds and the split of our spirit?

The answer to that question is entirely up to you. In fact, it can only be answered by you. Hopefully this book will stimulate the force of your inner wisdom and greatness to find the answer and to experience the union with yourself as you retrieve the sovereignty of your being.

Stanislav Grof, one of the greatest explorers of our time, searches the contents of the human psyche, diving into the deep waters of the unconscious and climbing the top of the mountains of the conscious experience of life. He explains to us the importance of mythology and myth for the human being and the human race in his paper *Archetypes, Mythic Imagination, and Modern Society*. Stan has been a pioneer for psychiatry and psychology, which is why many have not been able to understand or accept his findings, just like it was for Galileo Galilei or Albert Einstein. In fact, many years will probably pass before we can truly appreciate the gifts of his travels into the depths of human consciousness.

The following text is a tribute to one of the best storytellers who walked the Earth in the 20th century, Joseph Campbell:

"Follow your bliss.
The heroic life is living the individual adventure.
There is no security in following the call to adventure.
Nothing is exciting if you know what the outcome is going to be.
To refuse the call means stagnation.
What you don't experience positively you will experience
negatively.
You enter the forest at the darkest point, where there is no path.
Where there is a way or path, it is someone else's path.
You are not on your own path.
If you follow someone else's way, you are not going to realize
your potential.
The goal of the hero trip down to the jewel point is to find those
levels in the psyche that open, open, open and finally open to
the mystery of your Selfbeing Buddha consciousness or the
Christ.
That's the journey."
(Joseph Campbell)

"The choice is yours;
the choice for action or inaction is entirely
up 'you'.
'You' have the power to create universes
and cease universes.
The consequences of your actions or
inactions will be gathered by 'you',
and only 'you' will be answerable
to 'you' in the room of mirrors,
in Etznab's world,
before dissolving into emptiness."
Ná Áak

AWAKENING
CONSCIOUSNESS

Beyond
2012

Ná Áak
Paola Ambrosi

Section One
Wake Up Call

"When I think I know it all, I miss knowing it all. Only when I give myself permission to be ignorant, can I have moments of realisation beyond ignorance. If I am never ignorant then what is there to realise?"
Ná Áak

Chapter I
Acknowledging There is an Illness

We can have a better understanding of the world we live in if we can understand the people that created it. Let's tour the globe and have a look inside some different lives and catch a glimpse at how they think .....

Elena
...As I sit reading the newspaper I learn about a teenager that was raped and murdered a few miles down the road in an act of rage and violence after a night on the town with some friends. I change the page to see that a government minister has been implicated in fraud and may even be guilty of stealing. I do not like politics so I change the page to read that a film star has died of an overdose. The phone rings and interrupts my reading. It is my mother wanting to know when I am going to come home, my dad has not been well lately, he seemed fine until he was made redundant after 17 years with the company. This time she is giving out because her appointment with the hairdresser was cancelled. Honestly, I cannot be bothered listening to her going on and on about the same things. I am supposed to be working and my boss is expecting me to finish a presentation for the next meeting "Mum I have to go I am busy, talk later, bye" the sound of her voice was like a drill inside my head.

I I'll better get stuck into this presentation, my boss wants me to 're-focus' the results from the end of year accounts so they looks better for the potential investors Seems to me they are about to be ripped off. What do I care? It is my boss's responsibility; it is him who will burn in hell, if there is a hell.

The meeting was a success; we are going for a meal to celebrate. I hate these meals, they are all small talk and fake smiles the only good thing is that my boss is into good wine and he's paying.

Maybe I shouldn't have had that last glass of wine.

Oh, no! I am in bed naked with Mr Gaughan, the client. He is asleep, good! Maybe I can sneak out. Oh my head is killing me, always a sign I had one too many.

What time is it? 9pm, what! Seven missed calls from my husband. Where are my clothes? I can't believe I actually ended up in bed with this man. I don't even know him. Oh no, he is waking up! This is embarrassing and awkward. Where are my keys? Oh my bloody nail, they weren't cheap, so much for long lasting.

Peter
...I am sitting on the side of the road, life is unfair! How come I have so little and other people have so much? I am not a bad person. Where is god now Fr. Byrne, he is not showing his love in my world.

Sara
... Life is so unfair Norman my eldest comes out and says he is Gay! What a disappointment, I have no idea what got in his head. I still pray for him to find a cure...

Omar
...No food today, maybe tomorrow. Mum looks worried. Oh, look a piece of metal wire! I can make mum a flower, maybe she won't worry so much then. Perhaps it is worth something? who could I sell it to? I will just make her a flower it will be better to see her happy...

Lala
...Another day waiting by the window for Demba and Amar. They walk 2 miles to catch a bus that takes them to the nearest town where they go to school. I am worried about Amar, I think he is losing his sight. I better take him to those people at the tent at the other side of the village, they are doctors maybe they know what is wrong with my Amar. If it wasn't for the money from the charity we would be hungry today and Demba would have no shoes to walk to school...

I don't like this, the big trucks are coming, Amar! Demba! Where are you? I hope they don't cross paths with them, I better hide. Please god do not let them find Amar and Demba, please keep them safe. Oh no they are coming in...

"Where are you bitch!?"

I cannot hear anything anymore. I just feel the breath of a man on top of me and his gun. Please god keep Demba and Amar safe, please do not let them find them.

Everything is turning, I don't know if I can stand up...wait! My boys where are they? The trucks are leaving there is only dust and bodies. Please god, please where are my children?

"Lala, Lala, they took Demba! They took Demba!"
"What!? Where is Amar?"
He is dead!

Kamala
...Toward the One, the Perfection of Love, Harmony and Beauty, the Only Being, United with all the illuminated Souls, who form the Embodiment of the Master, the Spirit of Guidance... -too many capitals – leave only on Towards and One and Spirit

Philip
Looking out the window into the river, what a beautiful city this is but so many people, why am I feeling like this it was simply another meeting; protocol nothing else, why do I feel as if there is something wrong, what was different? Thomas gave the report as usual: "...these are the results from the tests done over the last number of years, all looks promising, and I would say that if this drug is introduced next month as planned you could have a return of the investment very quickly. There is only one concern that we need to deal with. The drug seemed to have caused mild blindness in some cases. What are you implying Thomas? Did you just say mild blindness? Yes, that is what I said; and did you just say in some cases? Yes. Mild blindness is not 'blindness' and 'some cases' shows that there is a very low risk to the vast majority As far as I am concerned I do not see a problem with this, do you gentlemen? A

unanimous 'No' came back. Good! Go ahead with the launch as planned...

Anah
... What is going to happen to us? Yesterday I had a home, today we have nothing! A refugee camp, what is that? I do not understand, but as my grandmother says "Do not ask questions to these men just do as they tell you". What are they doing here? This is not their country they do not even speak our language...

Rodrigo
...How do I tell her? We are only a few months from our baby being born. "Sandra I have to talk to you, I am joining the army. They promise good money for you and the baby in case anything happens to me. This can make all our dreams come true."...

Jóannes
...It is this time of the year again. I can't wait to get out there. What is the big deal? It is not as if I kill people, what is a couple of hundred whales?...

Adrian
... I trusted him, he was always good to me, but he touched me and I did not want that, he forced me!!... It is best for all concerned to get this resolved today, once you have signed the confidentially agreement we will issue the cheque and you can get on with your life. You do know that we are very sorry for what you have been put through. If you could just sign here...

Vanessa
...I am going mad, I think life is not worth living, this time I will do it I need this burning pain to end, I just want this pain to go away, please stop! Just go away!! Die!!...

Lu
...Om Mani Padme Hung, Rhi, Om Mani Padme Hung, Rhi, ...

George

...I am telling you we are going to war they attacked us, this cannot be left unpunished, and they will regret ever having placed a foot on our land...

Phia

...Om purna mada purna midam, Purnaat purnam udachyate Purnasya purnam adaaya, Purnam eva vasishyate, Om shanti shanti shantih...

Oja

...Mum, No. I told you I do not want to marry him, I love Kala. Do you hear that! I love Kala; I have always loved her...

Antonio

...Modeh ani l'fanecha melech chai v'kayam sh'hechezarta bi nishmati b'chemla rabah emunatecha...

Rebeca

...why is it me that always has to give the bad news? Ok let's get on with it and not think too much about it..."Mrs Gaughan I have the results of your biopsy, you have cancer, I am sorry". I hope she does not start crying now! I could not cope with that ...

Susana

...how do I tell my mum I am pregnant? She will kill me! No, I cannot ever tell her. I will make this go away but where do I go? Just goggle abortion! Come on Susana, do not be paranoid just check it on the internet and do it! What if it is alive already? Could that be possible? It can't be that hard, well if I think it is alive...? I am talking to myself, this can't be good...

Luna

...The Great Spirit is in all things, is in the air we breathe. The Great Spirit is our Father, but the Earth is our Mother. She nourishes us; that which we put into the ground, she returns to us....

"Because what does not exist appears delusion
Provides the cause for completely afflicted states;
Since things like illusory elephants appear,
Even what does exist does not appear.
If either the lack of existence or the appearance
Were missing, delusion and freedom from
delusion
And likewise states afflicted in every respect
And thorough refinement would be unjustified."
(Maitreya)

Elena

Elena had two children and worked at the bank until she retired. After a sudden and serious illness her children made the decision to switch off the life support machine. Mr. Gaughan the man she slept with lost big money investing in Elena's bosses bank. After the death of his wife he fell into deep depression and tried to kill himself. He was sectioned in a psychiatric unit and died after one of many Electro Convulsive Therapy treatments.

Peter

Peter lived on the streets until one day he was around the wrong area at the wrong time and the police picked him up as a murder suspect. He was sent to prison for manslaughter. He never even knew the victim.

Sara

Sara died in the arms of her son Norman, the son she never accepted.

Omar

Omar died a week after he made the flower for his mum. She smiled every time she saw it and on her death it was put in the grave with her.

Lala

Lala moved town after burying her son and found a job in a factory where she worked quietly until she died peacefully in her sleep. She knew she would meet Amar and Demba at the other side.

Kamala

...Toward the One the Perfection of Love, Harmony and Beauty, the Only Being, United with all the illuminated Souls, who form the Embodiment of the Master, the Spirit of Guidance...

Philip

Philip worked and lived for the company until at 53 he had a heart attack in a taxi on his way from somewhere to somewhere. He died alone. The company had replaced him and moved on within weeks of his funeral

Anah
Anah joined the armed movement in her country. She fought and thanks to her and many like her the drilling for oil stopped for some time. She was captured and executed as a terrorist.

Rodrigo
Rodrigo never came back from war. The money as compensation was never paid, the country was going through a recession. Rodrigo Junior eventually found a job in a fast food chain to help his mum.

Jóannes
Jóannes continued with his tradition of killing whales and died as a result of a bad fall he had at the docks during the celebrations of the annual festival.

Adrian
Adrian found ways of overcoming the abuse and after many disastrous relationships he married. The nightmares never stopped but he died in the arm of the woman he loved.

Vanessa
Vanessa killed herself after many attempts. In her note she wrote:"Why did you not listen to me?"

Lu
...Om Mani Padme Hung, Rhi, Om Mani Padme Hung, Rhi,...

George
George was promoted and made prime minister of the country; many saw opportunity in a new war. The war was fought many died but the country recovered financially and many invested in gold, oil, and property in the country they won. He lives happily with his wife and children, at his funeral there will be a service of honour.

Phia

...Om purna mada purna midam, Purnaat purnam udachyate Purnasya purnam adaaya, Purnam eva vasishyate, Om shanti shanti shantih...

Oja

Oja and Kala left their town and started a new life. They set up a rescue facility for children where they helped people smile again. They both died at peace although none of their families were present.

Antonio

...Modeh ani l'fanecha melech chai v'kayam sh'hechezarta bi nishmati b'chemla rabah emunatecha...

Rebeca

Rebeca practiced as a medical doctor all her life. She had good holidays and drove good cars. When death came to visit it was cancer and only then she understood why people cried when they realize they were ill and the idea of death became very real. She died scared after spending all her savings in unsuccessful treatments.

Susana

Susana kept her baby. Her and her daughter had fun and enjoyed life. One day in her old age she was stabbed on the street as a burglar stole her purse.

Luna

...The Great Spirit is in all things, is in the air we breathe. The Great Spirit is our Father, but the Earth is our Mother. She nourishes us; that which we put into the ground, she returns to us...

Xa jun e k'o wi
Ki kaj ichal.

Xeb'ixanik.
Chi q'atat ki k'u'x.

Choq' pu ki k'u'x
Chupan ki b'ixik.

"Qa Muqu" u b'i' ki b'ix
Xkib'ixaj.
(Popol Vuh)

Only one they are
The four of them.
They sang
Of affliction their hearts.
They would weep as well their hearts
Within their song.
"Our Burial" its name their song
They sang
(Popol Vuh)

> *My thoughts, my speech and my actions are my song.*
> *What I think, what I say and what I do is my musical masterpiece.*
> *Ná Áak*

When music is made, many different instruments, sounds and silences are used to produce a melody to flow through us and enchant the heart. The rhythm of the music becomes the 'tick-tock' behind the masterpiece. All those playing the different instruments have to follow this rhythm for the melody to take shape. It is a hidden map. The rhythm plays throughout the musical masterpiece. The tick-tock in the background becomes the guide, helping the musicians to play together at an agreed pace.

Along with the common rhythm, every instrument has its own score, indicating the notes to play and, most important, indicating the silences. This is the plan that each instrument will follow to make its contribution at the required time.

The conductor opens the session and a beautiful combination of harmonics, rhythm, silence, percussion, strings, wind instruments and piano can be enjoyed. When the music flows it resonates inside our bodies; it lifts our spirit; it triggers emotion inside us and it can be blissful and mystical.

After listening to the different voices of our world above, what rhythm or symphony does it seem to you that we are playing right now on this Earth?

The natural survival and defence mechanism that we default to after experiencing horror is denial.

Denial sounds like this: "It is not real, it did not happen, it cannot be true, it is impossible, unrealistic, and crazy. It has not been proven scientifically or statistically correct or true."

We have created many thousands of escape routes into denial. All that is an inconvenient reality in our world gets erased, cut off, put in a box labelled "bad", "wrong" or "anti-institutional", dismissed, locked away in psychiatric wards or prisons or it gets executed.

We silence the voices that speak of freedom, peace, liberation, equality and democracy. We have become so afraid of anything challenging the 'institution' that we charge against those voices like a terrified rhinoceros, without asking questions. We simply shoot and kill.

When we have chosen denial as a way of living we are prepared to do everything it takes to preserve our illusion and to keep our reality safe. The 'institution' is your social and cultural handbook, your faith, your beliefs and all you accept as real and 'true' for you. This idea of 'institution' applies to the world outside yourself, the 'institution' becoming the banks, political parties, church, family, etc.; and it applies also to the world inside you. The 'institutions' inside yourself are your thoughts, your emotions. It is the personalised conditioning that you carry as a human being from before, during and after you were conceived by your parents.

When we live in denial we might be experiencing symptoms of the illness but we choose not to look into them or find their cause. We simply experience isolated events and decide to ignore or gloss over them.

An easy way to understand this can be looking into our emotions. Have you ever felt that life was not worth living? And what exactly did you do with that feeling? Was it taken to action? Did you forget about it? Or did you choose to ignore it because you were afraid of what would happen if you let it speak loud and clear?

The feelings that come up are simply the red lights of the body telling us that something is happening inside and outside ourselves. When I feel life is not worth living, I am only feeling the tip of the iceberg of what is really happening inside and outside of me. We can choose to dive into the water and discover the rest of the iceberg, and find a way of helping that iceberg to melt into the ocean; or we can choose to refuse to admit that there is an iceberg.

But the iceberg will not disappear. It will remain there unseen and denied. We find ways to navigate around it, and we learn to avoid hitting it, but it will be there as we wake up every day and it will still be there on the day we meet our death.

When we look into the struggle and turmoil that happens every second inside our minds, we hear a disharmonic loud sound with no rhythm, no flow and no silences. Sometimes the sounds are of fear, of terror, horror at life circumstances like Lala, Anah or Adrian's story, sometimes we hear emptiness and blindness like in Elena's and Rebecca's story, sometimes, despair and frustration like in Vanessa's story.

What do you hear when you listen to you your own story?

Our society is ill. It is out of balance.

The evidence is inside us and all around us. When I hear a mother crying because her daughter of only 11 years of age has hung herself from her bedroom door, I do not have to question whether we, as a community, are out of balance and in disharmony with nature, I know we are. The sound of our inner and outer turmoil and suffering is making our children kill themselves.

The tune of a healthy Earth is long gone and at times I find it very hard to know what is playing instead. When I hear the disharmony my chest hurts, my bones burn in pain and my tears become insufficient to express the horror of the hell I hear. My heart explodes in a painful silent scream of rage.

We have lost connection with the reality we have created collectively. We are numb to each other's pain as a consequence of being numb to our own pain. We have lost respect for life and living because we have lost respect for our own selves. We believe that all that happens is someone else's fault. We blame others to wash away our own guilt. We take no personal responsibility for our actions, and most importantly, we take no personal responsibility for our *inactions*.

15

We need to wake up from our lethargy and anaesthesia. How can we say there is balance, equality and 'democracy' in the world when some people are concerned about fake nails and others watch their child being cut open by a machete; when some people are spending money on plastic surgery and others spend it to silence a child that was sexually abused; when some people are concerned about getting the colouring of their hair right and others grieve a loved one that committed suicide; when some people are buying a new car while others are dying of starvation; when some people are hunting for pleasure and others are killing human beings because they have a different colour or religion; when some people are having abortions while others are searching frantically for their missing child.

To me this sound is neither harmonious nor rhythmic. No matter how much perfume is sprayed over it, the smell of blood does not fade away.

> *"For an event to possess greatness two things must come together: greatness of spirit in those who accomplish it and greatness of spirit in those who experience it. No event possesses greatness in itself, though it involve the disappearance of whole constellations, the destruction of entire peoples, the foundation of vast states or the prosecution of wars involving tremendous forces and tremendous losses: the breath of history has blown away many things of that kind as though they were flakes of snow."*
> *(Nietzsche)*

Chapter II
The Illness

> 'Illness – Impairment of normal functioning
> of a part or all of an organism.'

If we can expand our understanding of life beyond denial, then we can open the door for healing. Until then we are at the mercy of the illness.

When we look around us it might seem that there are many different illnesses and mutations of the virus. It might feel overwhelming, listening to the sound of disharmony. If we allow ourselves to really see the suffering around us, we might want to fight harder to stop it, or we might want to run away. This is a natural response of nature when confronted with 'trauma' or a painful experience, we fight or we fly. It is an animal survival instinct and it operates within us to protect us and preserve life.

This reaction happens over and over again inside and outside. When it happens outside you might find yourself in the middle of a fist fight or in a screaming match with someone if you're reaction is to fight; or if your reaction is flight, you might run away, go into hiding, or just become very silent.

When this happens in the inside you might experience the fight turning against you and therefore you become your worst enemy by blaming yourself, feeling guilt, hate or simply giving out to yourself in your own mind. When we react by flight, what happens inside is that we become absent, we disappear, we disconnect and dissociate from our physical, emotional or intellectual body. We fly outside of ourselves.

When these reactions are out of control the fight survival response can turn into a paranoid or obsessive compulsive behaviour, for example, incapacitating us to do anything because we are in a constant internal battle. Or it may make us an aggressive person unable to contain anger. The flight response in its extreme form might take us, for example, into depression as there is no one present in the here and now in our bodies because we have effectively flown away.

These are responses that we all have to life circumstances. Each one of us responds one way or another depending on our conditioning and awareness. It is very easy to get lost in the rollercoaster of life and the drama of living. It is actually very tempting to look into the stories of life and get consumed by misery and pain. We learn to engage in the drama from an early age and as time passes there comes a point when we completely forget who we are and become the drama itself. We become the depression, or the cancer, or the guilt, or the abuse or the misery. We lose our centre and then we live on automatic pilot, driven blindly by our conditioning into more of the same depression, cancer, abuse, abandonment, etc.

We live in a realm of experience and perceptual interpretation of the experience. We receive stimuli through our senses; our brain processes the stimuli; it categorises it by comparing it with previous experiences stored in our memory bank, and then it shouts a response to the experience.

It is our nature to experience the world, to feel it, to smell it, to touch it. We are sentient beings. The physical machinery that we have evolved into is a perfect receptor of infinite frequencies. Pleasure and pain are part of the spectrum of frequencies that we can perceive and experience. When you think about something, you do not only receive the frequency and are able to name it, but as you receive it something magical happens. You can experience the frequency that you are receiving. This is part of the beauty of a human experience - the capacity to experience life in full in the here and now with no delay.

As we gain experiences and information in our sophisticated receiver we condition ourselves to activate certain responses. We associate a colour with a shape, or a shape with a feeling, or a person with a meaning. For example, if right now I say.....

"RED"

......you immediately have a reaction to it. You were given a visual or a feeling by your brain, or maybe even thought of a person or a situation. I am sure that if we could compare our thoughts with each other we would find elements in common which, in itself, constitutes our collective conditioning.

This collective conditioning develops according to our Socio-Cultural-Political-Religious experiences and background. Then we have individual conditioning, which is the unique association that each one of us can have with RED. This association belongs to our unique personal experience of life including all that happened before, during and after conception, as we mentioned before.

Both the collective and individual experiences and information stores are active at all times in our receptor and are continuously giving us information about every single moment we experience in life. This conditioned reaction cannot be switched off. It continuously runs in the background consciously and unconsciously, just like a program in a computer. Sometimes we are aware that a program has opened in the computer and is processing information, but more often we remain unaware of the many programs running in the background.

Let's entertain some ideas. What would happen if I tell you that RED equals evil; It represents evil; it is evil and it means evil. In fact, let's imagine I am your mother or your father and you ask me: what is RED? "RED is evil and you should never be close to it or relate to it in any way. Remember it is evil, stay away from it!"

As time goes by you meet a man that is RED, and against all the instructions you have been given you cannot help but to fall in love with the RED man. Your parents disapprove because RED means evil and they let you know that it is not in your best interest to be around RED. Because they love you they forbid you to be with this man, and say that you must never see RED again.

You might have ignored this and decided to run away with RED man, or maybe you obeyed their wishes and left RED man, never to discover if RED meant anything other than evil.

What happens if I am a policeman investigating a murder? I interview YELLOW, BLUE and RED Whether I am conscious of this or not my mind will work as it is supposed to and will send me the message that 'RED = evil'. I will impartially review the information that YELLOW and BLUE gave to me, but for some unknown reason, I have a bad feeling about RED. I might even decide that RED is the murderer.

What happens if I am someone in a powerful position in government? Perhaps there is a country that has a lot of RED people and they are immigrating to my country of GREEN people. They eat RED, they dress RED, they pray RED, they are RED! Since I 'know' that 'RED = evil' I won't tolerate this in my GREEN country, so I decide to get rid of the RED and deport them; or maybe treat them badly so they decide to leave by themselves; or maybe I will just kill them and have a RED-free world, where it is anti-constitutional to be RED.

What happens if I am a religious leader conditioned with the same message that 'RED = evil'? All that is RED is outside the bounds of the 'Lord' and my YELLOW church; RED is inconvenient and primitive; it is the work of the 'devil'. But because I am a merciful man I will teach my YELLOW people to take the REDness out of the RED so they can have a chance of salvation and become YELLOW. Then they will find grace and a place in our one and only true YELLOW heaven. Those who refuse to turn YELLOW must be eliminated.

If we were to stay congruent and objective, would we say that this would be a fair way to educate children, or run a country or lead a religion?

I can only guess, but I am sure that at least more than one of you disagrees with the statement:

RED = evil

How can we decide, then, who has the right to create a definition of RED or which interpretation is the true, correct and irrevocable meaning of RED?

If what has been explained before does not make much sense to you or maybe seems childish and simplistic then just replace the word RED for black, or muslim, or gay or native or whatever word is relevant in your society.

The Story of the RAINBOW People

There was a time when the RAINBOW people inhabited the Earth. They danced and sang all the seven colours of the rainbow. The sky would rain and the light would shine through the drops of rain filling the Earth with the RAINBOW, full of COLOUR. Each colour had a tune that they would play, as they gathered together they would sing and play each unique tune in harmony. The RAINBOW would get strong and bright and all the Earth would become one.

One day the Light whispered: "times of darkness will come when you will be pulled apart, when you will fight against each other and kill and torture each other. Times will come when you will forget you once were equal, when you will forget that you once were a RAINBOW. Those will be times of pain and sorrow for you all, but you must not forget you are a RAINBOW, you have always been a RAINBOW and you can always be a RAINBOW again. There is little you can do about this. The tick-tock of the universe is moving towards the pole of separation and differentiation. But it is part of your journey to separate and experience the loneliness of not being a RAINBOW and being an alone COLOUR. You can always be a RAINBOW again but not until you die completely to your COLOUR, immerse yourself in Darkness and emerge from that COLOURLESNESS into your new RAINBOWNESS. What is needed of you to survive this experience is to be unafraid and remember that what you are seeing is only the wheel of the universe spinning from Darkness into Light. It has always spun this way and it will eternally spin from one pole to the other. Those who forget where their centre is will perish and lose themselves in fear. Those who know how to anchor their hearts to the centre of the wheel will never be lost. Do not fear what is natural; do not fear who you are; do not ever fear Death. Do not ever fear Darkness."

In horror the COLOURS spoke to each other and tried to decide the best way to pass this information from generation to generation so that no one would get lost. They prepared calendars and wheels of cycles pointing out the crucial times in the process that the Light described. They carved the symbols and their meanings in stone so that the weather would not destroy the message over time. They wrote scriptures and prophecies describing who they were and how they lived. They created practices that would help them always remember who they were. The elders agreed to continuously reincarnate on Earth to lead the way and help others remember until all were out of Darkness.

One day GREEN had a moment of revelation where it felt things it had not felt before. That morning GREEN felt very GREEN and experienced itself thinking "I am GREEN." It realised then that all of the other colours were different, and for a moment it desired what they had. The next day it felt angry for the first time because it was GREEN and not RED. It felt jealous of how vibrant RED always appeared and how dull GREEN seemed. The day after that it experienced regret for not being RED and felt depressed about how GREEN it was. As it reflected on its feelings it realised that maybe everybody could turn against RED and that they would hate RED forever. It then realized that it could then have what RED had and in a moment of greed it wondered what would happen if it did that to all the other COLOURS. The next morning it started planning how to turn everyone against RED, but very quickly it realised that RED could come over and fight back and turn everyone against GREEN! It felt afraid. Its fear made it even more ruthless about his plan against RED, reasoning that there could be no loose ends.

So the campaign started, and slowly everyone started mistrusting RED. The anger, jealousy, greed, depression, desire and fear that had overcome GREEN quickly spread into ORANGE, YELLOW, BLUE, INDIGO, and VIOLET, leaving RED alone and isolated. RED became synonymous with evil and everyone helped to keep evil under control.

Years passed and our ancestors grew up knowing and learning about the evil that was RED. They witnessed wars against RED; they saw their RED friends being converted or killed; they heard religious and political leaders preaching about the horrors of RED and the bad things that could happen to you if you look into RED or thought RED or spoke RED. New generations were born and they immediately knew to stay clear of RED and peace reigned in a RED-free world.

But RED was always a colour of the rainbow of the Earth and it could not be exterminated completely. In spite of some being imprisoned, others being killed and others converted it was impossible to make RED disappear. Every so often, a burst of RED would happen giving the others reason for another war or more extermination.

Because of fear, GREEN made sure that all traces of the Light's warning about RAINBOW people and the times to come was destroyed. Any elder who remembered was killed, and it became anti-GREEN and blasphemy to speak the word RAINBOW.

Some got so used to life without RED that when it emerged again they thought nothing of supporting the campaign against RED because they believed that the rainbow only had six colours and RED was an aberration of nature. A rainbow with RED did not exist, it was anti-natural. There was no trace or memory of the whispers of the Light or the times of the RAINBOW people.

Some were so tired of the conflicts with RED that they reinforced the original belief from their ancestors to the point that they would do anything to stop RED, even if it meant disowning their own children.

Those who never forgot RED and those who continued to feel a burst of RED inside had to live in the shadows.

Those who were RED had to tolerate horrible torture, massacre, killing, abuse, extradition. In their collective memory all of this pain and injustice were carved into their RED bones like you would carve stone. As new generations were born the anger and rage of what they had endured kept building up in their RED hearts and they too forgot that they were once part of the RAINBOW of the Earth. The injustice and the pain made them forget they were more than only RED and they over-identified with being the persecuted COLOUR. So generations came to believe that the COLOUR of the world was determined by who ruled the world. Some RED built up so much resentment that they dreamed about a world that was only RED, a world for RED people and RED life where no other colour would be allowed to shine. They dreamed of a future where they could be in control and show the other colours what they were made of.

This is the story of how the RAINBOW people forgot they were a RAINBOW. They were sad times. Just as the Light had whispered, each colour separated itself to protect its COLOURNESS. One by one, RED, ORANGE, YELLOW, GREEN, BLUE, INDIGO and VIOLET found its own place to live and its own ideas to believe. Never happy with what they had, they were constantly fighting against each other for more land, more power, more control, always living in fear of one another. It is said that the sky cried so much in the times of NO-RAINBOW, that it flooded the Earth with black tears.

Never again would its rain reflect a rainbow because the colours never again wanted to be near each other.

At times, just as the elders promised to each other, wise men and women would come into being reminding the COLOUR people that they were not just COLOUR people but that they were RAINBOW people. Very few understood and listened. Many came and many were silenced because to accept that they were RAINBOW people would compromise all that each COLOUR lived and fought for, their independence and power.

As time passed and old wounds from the past began to heal, many believed that a RAINBOW Earth could be born again. They sang RAINBOW people songs and dreamed of a RAINBOW world.

At the head of the COLOUR government there was now a challenge. More and more people had new information and were beginning to remember their capacity to be a RAINBOW. It was harder to fight this because it was no longer RED or YELLOW but it was coming from all the colours - RED, ORANGE, YELLOW, GREEN, BLUE, INDIGO and VIOLET. All the colours started mixing with one another and becoming friends and the government faced new troubles in this mixture of COLOURS. The YELLOW were learning GREEN so they wanted to be YELLOW-GREEN and the ORANGE began to learn VIOLET and wanted to be ORANGE-VIOLET, and so on.

After much thought, a solution came to protect the position of power that each colour had achieved. COLOUR was to be banned! All the Earth was to be GREY, speak GREY, eat GREY, and dress GREY. Imagine the potential? If we join forces in GREY we can not only profit from YELLOW but also from GREEN, BLUE, RED, etc. This GREY idea would facilitate communication and make things easier to control.

As generations were born into the GREY world they started forgetting they ever had a COLOUR and of course there was no trace of ever being a RAINBOW. There was a vague

25

recollection of the RAINBOW movement far away in old times when music was made from instruments and when people spoke face to face. Now life is simple, life is GREY! We send messages through machines and we all speak GREY.

Sometimes a rumour circulated that elders from the RAINBOW people would reincarnate in times of GREY to help people remember. But fear and greed became so ingrained in the GREY world that the GREY people could not even hear anything that was not GREY. But these elders continued to repeat in every RED, ORAGNE, YELLOW, GREEN, BLUE, INDIGO, VIOLET and GREY the whispers of the Light:

"...You can always be a RAINBOW again but not until you die completely to your COLOUR, immerse yourself in Darkness and emerge from that COLOURLESNESS into your new RAINBOWNESS. What is needed of you to survive this experience is to be unafraid and remember that what you are seeing is only the wheel of the universe spinning from Darkness into Light. It has always spun this way and it will eternally spin from one pole to the other. Those who forget where their centre is will perish and lose themselves in fear. Those who know how to anchor their hearts to the centre of the wheel will never be lost. Do not fear what is natural; do not fear who you are; do not ever fear Death; do not ever fear Darkness."

It is said that when the time came some people listened and remembered their COLOURNESS. They allowed it to die in the darkness and they emerged from the Emptiness as a radiant RAINBOW. Others never came out of the darkness. Fear took hold of them and took them deeper into the world of fearful illusions. Others remembered their COLOURNESS and decided to reinforce it and fight for a GREEN or ORANGE or YELLOW world, taking many with them into conflicts that were to last for years, bringing starvation and illness. Some said that GREY fought for control over the COLOUR and used big weapons that made the COLOUR fade away in people, making them numb and blind to colour. It was said that at one point GREY used a machine that made millions of people disappear into a ball of blinding light and silence. Others lived blissfully ignorant in GREY, not ever knowing that there was anything different to life. It is said, though, that the whisper of the Light came true and the tick-tock of the Universe started swinging away from darkness into the Light, causing everything to collapse and re-creating a new Earth where RAINBOWS could shine.

We do not really know what happened. Maybe it all happened or maybe nothing happened, or maybe this is only a story..."

There is only one illness we are dancing with:

IGNORANCE

The symptoms are vast and, in cases, unique to each individual situation. But the core of our illness as GREY people is the ignorance about our true RAINBOW nature. The syndrome that is behind our misfortune and suffering is our apathy and indifference towards life. Not wanting to realise that our actions as much as our inactions have big consequences and that there is no one out there to blame for our misery or the misery of the world but ourselves.

We have been indoctrinated to believe there is only one truth -each person has their own, similar to the example of RED=evil, and that truth is irrevocable and cannot be questioned. From that perspective, and adding many other factors that we will explore in the next section, we believe as human beings that "we know it all." I have my truth and that is all I want to know because that is all there is to know. The idea of even considering another possible truth is criminal, just as it was for the Colour people who thought that a rainbow had only six colours and to even consider that RED was part of it was an aberration. That is Ignorance. That is how Ignorance holds us as its slaves. In ignorance we cannot see; we are blind we are not awake although we claim we have full vision. In some respect we do have full vision, but only of what we want to see or what we can see.

Ignorance is when we dance blindly with anger, desire, greed, jealousy, depression and fear. These states of consciousness take hold of us and control our reactions and our actions; they make us forget the bigger picture of who we are and they separate us from the whole. When we dance with them in ignorance they are in control. We need to learn to dance with them awake so they can be observed and experienced in their polar opposites: compassion, discernment, introspection, generosity, detachment and wisdom.

How can we read a new book and take in what is offered if we are already full and in the understanding that "I know it all already." When we engage in life with that perspective there is nothing we learn and we are simply fooling ourselves that we are changing when in fact we see no effect of the change. That is Ignorance dancing with us again.

Do we really want to learn and expand beyond our limitations as the many self-help books promise? Then stop being GREY and find out what and who you really are. Connect with those who walked before you and see the world through the eyes of RED, ORANGE, YELLOW, GREEN, BLUE, INDIGO or VIOLET. Find your COLOUR tribe; reconnect with its tradition, with its life and then let it all go. Surrender to Death, letting your "I AMness" die. It is in that moment, and only in the moment of crossing the bridge of 'Death' that we can be reborn. All has its own cycle and spiral of evolution and so does internal and external growth, individually and collectively. Follow the cycle, let go, embrace Death to embrace Life.

The only way to awaken from Ignorance is by fully accepting:

"I am ignorant"

"The fool who knows he is a fool
Is that much wiser.
The fool who thinks he is wise
Is a fool indeed.

Does the spoon taste the soup?
A fool may live all his life
In the company of a master
And still miss the way.

The tongue tastes the soup
If you are awake in the presence of a master
One moment will show you the way.

The fool is his own enemy.
The mischief he does is his undoing.
How bitterly he suffers!"
(Dhammapada)

Chapter III
The Power of the Illness

Now that we can name the illness.....

" I am Ignorant"

.....we can look at the power that being ignorant has in our world and also in our internal reality.

The effects of Ignorance can be perceived as gross or subtle. The gross effects are the loudest and most visible signs and the subtle effects are the small and almost invisible manifestations of the illness.

The gross effects are easy to point out and therefore they are easy to treat because they are large and visible. They are the signs that we cannot miss even if we wanted to. When we can see clearly we can apply a direct solution to resolve the imbalance. But what happens then with the subtle effects? When we cannot see clearly and walk in darkness how can we point out what is really happening? It is because of this that the subtle effects are sometimes more dangerous than the gross effects, they are more difficult to resolve because they are more difficult to find and acknowledge.

We will explain in detail the human psyche as we go along, but for now I want to introduce two basic concepts of human existence:

Conscious
Unconscious

Let's assume that the human being is an iceberg floating in deep waters. The conscious aspect of human existence is the part of you that is aware and awake to life and to yourself. This is the part of the human experience that emerges above the water becoming the visible tip of the iceberg. Your conscious self can read these lines and understand what you are reading. It is the present self. It is the self that knows what, how and why it is doing something. It is the part of you that lives in the now, in the present moment.

The unconscious aspect of you is the aspect of the human existence that remains covered underneath the water. It is the rest of the unseen iceberg of who you are. It is this part of the self and your being that contains the information of every single life experience and serves as a big *hard drive* full of information, constantly feeding and directing the conscious experience.

When I refer to conscious self I mean the whole of you who is conscious to your life experience, and when I refer to unconscious self it means the whole of your human experience that is unknown to you in which case it would include the iceberg below the water and the water itself. The iceberg that is invisible to you is your individual unconscious and the waters that are unknown to you represent your collective unconscious. The concept of the collective unconscious was introduced to psychology by Carl Jung around the 1950's, together with many other ideologies that have created the foundation of modern psychology, but we will explore in detail the human psyche in later chapters.

The visible part of the iceberg, which rises above the water, is the conscious self, displaying to you the gross effects of ignorance. Below the water, the invisible part of the iceberg is the unconscious self displaying the subtle effects of ignorance. This is a simplistic way of perceiving the human psyche but it is of great aid to start understanding how are we formed and how the sophisticated machine we call 'human being' operates.

What is conscious, obvious and known to me is not necessarily conscious, obvious and known to you. Each iceberg above the surface is unique and different, different parts of its totality are uncovered and its shape, size and form are unique. Our ability to map reality depends on the awareness and knowledge that we have of our own iceberg; the awareness and knowledge that we have about other icebergs and the awareness and knowledge that we have about the water. This means that each one of us will have a completely different experience of life. What I know is what becomes real and relevant to me. What I do not know becomes either insignificant or irrelevant to me. The way we consciously perceive reality becomes the way our reality gets shaped. This translates in simple terms as what I perceive to be real is real and what do I not perceive does not exist.

According to this perception of the icebergs and the water we can map different states of awareness. We will explore in general terms what this means with some examples of different realities:

COTTON reality

In the COTTON reality people are sitting on the tip of their iceberg, never realising they are an iceberg. They are simply floating on the surface of the water, just like floating in cotton clouds, never coming down to the solid ground. Icebergs living in this reality never know or want to know where they are, who they are and what all of this is about. It is a placid, peaceful place where nobody is disturbed and everyone is comfortably asleep. The advantage to this way of living is blissful ignorance. Icebergs living in COTTON reality only become aggressive when their sleep is disturbed; then they collectively drown the disturbance with sarcasm and humiliation.

An individual living in the COTTON reality gets upset and suffers if their car gets scratched or if their favourite soap opera goes off the air. They attack only if an iceberg from another reality questions their reaction.

ROCK reality

In the ROCK reality icebergs know they are icebergs and they are aware that there are other icebergs, but they can only see the ones that are similar or equal to them. They walk on firm land, solid, definite. They know they are made from ice; they know the composition of ice; they know the functions of ice. For these icebergs the water does not exist because it is not solid and measurable. In this place icebergs are knowledgeable and respectable. Their talent is their intellectual strength but they are stubborn. When another iceberg from another reality challenges their knowledge, introducing the idea of water or other possible icebergs of different shape, form or colour, they get very angry. They show their anger with disregard and attack the other iceberg with quotations and references from their own ROCK scriptures, constitutions and manuals. When Galileo introduced heliocentrism, stating that the Sun was at the centre of the universe and not the Earth, he was probably denounced by icebergs living in the ROCK reality. His theory was condemned as false and contrary to scripture.

PAPER reality

In the PAPER reality icebergs know they are icebergs, they have full awareness that there are other icebergs equal and different to them and they know about the water, but they have no idea what to do with this information. They find reality overwhelming and because they are scattered and afraid they have no grounding, bending just like paper. They get torn, written over and they disintegrate when they come in contact with the water. The strength of icebergs living in the PAPER reality is their flexibility. But their gift turns into a disadvantage when in fear they adopt the form of another iceberg to find security. They change depending on what iceberg offers the more apparent security, having no back bone of their own. Once they attach to another iceberg they fearsomely protect it because they depend on it to survive. When they are immersed in fear they become deaf to any other opinion, they are the ones that sink with the boat because they cannot afford to believe that the boat is sinking. Once I had an interesting conversation with an iceberg living in the PAPER reality, following a conversation with a group about the sexual abuse that occurred in the community. I said: "it must have been difficult to find out that the priest that you served for years was abusing so many children you personally knew." One iceberg abruptly responded:"maybe I doubted for a while when I first heard the news, but I know now it was all lies, young ones these days look for it anyway." I had nothing more to say.

FEATHER reality

In the FEATHER reality icebergs get tired of the iceberg reality and become absorbed by the nature of water. They become divers, going deep and far and in the wonder of this experience, they get lost in the water leaving their iceberg empty. They become explorers of the unknown but they never come back to tell their stories or to do something with their insight and knowledge. Just as feathers, they are taken away by the currents of the water, never returning to inhabit their iceberg. Their ability to go deeper and farther is admirable, but we never know what they have seen because their icebergs are still empty. Once, talking to an iceberg in recovery from heroin use, I understood some aspects of the FEATHER reality: "You have to see the beauty of the water. It is so soft and warm, it is gentle and it has no boundaries. But when I am in the iceberg I crash into other icebergs. I break and crack and feel horrible pain. When I am in the water I don't break and I don't feel pain." For years I didn't meet this iceberg until one day I received a phone call. After years of trying to inhabit his iceberg again, he eventually gave up and jumped again into the water, only this time he could not come back.

GOLD reality

In the GOLD reality the icebergs are aware of the whole reality of iceberg and water. But one thing fascinates them more than anything else: uncovering the iceberg that lies under the water. They thrive with the curiosity of all they do not know, and dedicate their lives to dig deep, to excavate the iceberg, to break it into pieces and to analyse every little discovery. Just as it was during the 'gold fever' in the olden days in America, icebergs in this reality get obsessed by digging for gold. The result is that their findings make an important contribution to the iceberg world, and this is always a huge catalyst for evolution. The down side is that, although they are experts in analysing the material they discover, they completely forget about life in iceberg world and most of the time they feel incapable of committing to social responsibilities. An iceberg living in the GOLD reality that changed the history of physics was Einstein. His findings on atomic energy and mass-energy equivalence, together with many other insights, set the template for the quantum science that exists today. On the other hand, he had a poor, almost non-existent relationship with his sons. His youngest son Eduard was diagnosed with schizophrenia and became a victim of the unscrupulous psychiatric care of those days.

DIAMOND Reality

In the DIAMOND reality icebergs are aware of all that is in solid ground, but accidentally or intentionally dive into the deep waters, learning to love the water as much as the iceberg life. Skilfully they learn the art of diving deep and coming back. They enjoy the pleasure and pain of both worlds - the iceberg world and the aquatic world. Their skill facilitates them to help others that have fallen into the water or that are afraid of the water. They are also skilful in helping other icebergs in iceberg world. They shine like diamonds and they allow the light to shine through them. They are as solid as diamonds and they are 'wanted' like diamonds. Insecurity is a flaw that can cause them to struggle, when in the need for approval they want to share their discoveries with others, making PAPER icebergs nervous or ROCK icebergs angry. Many times, because they are 'wanted' just like diamonds, they are eliminated because they become a threat to other icebergs living in other realities. Many great icebergs have passed through the DIAMOND reality such as Mahatma Gandhi, John Lennon, Benazir Bhutto, Alberto Che Guevara, and all those who lived for the community, served the community and dedicated their lives to help one another.

There are as many states of awareness as human beings, because although there are general aspects in common that can be mapped, there is something unique in each iceberg that can never be duplicated. This is the magic of this life experience: it is similar but never the same. There is so much perfection and beauty in the iceberg realities and in the water itself that I can only be in absolute AWE of creation.

At different times we all have the capacity to come in and out of the different realities and it is our choice which reality we decide to inhabit most of the time.

There is one more reality that I would like to include but that I always like keep separate from the rest because its poison spreads like fire in petrol. This is the IRON reality.

IRON reality
In the IRON reality the icebergs sit comfortably watching all that surrounds them, always afraid of exploring their iceberg, other icebergs or the water. These icebergs, in their inability to move, feed on other icebergs' attention and approval. They love to lecture others on how to explore and live, even though they themselves

have never explored or lived. They thrive on other icebergs' misery and suffering and enjoy pushing them into the water, demanding that they fetch the answers for them to prove their theories and cover up their inactivity. Although they appear to be full of knowledge, they are unlike the icebergs living in ROCK reality because they are not interested in knowing, but only in appearing as if they know. They live on fear, anger, jealousy, depression, desire and greed.

In this reality fear spreads like an infection, keeping other icebergs in delusion and denial because if one iceberg wakes up they might find out about the lies they have been told and they cannot afford to lose face to the world of icebergs. Out of fear of being discovered as a fraud the icebergs in the IRON reality have a crucial need to create dogma, constitutions and manuals to establish a set of rules about iceberg correct and incorrect behaviour, about what is right and what is wrong for every iceberg.

The imperative is to keep other icebergs from discovering their lies. In order to fulfil their need they ban books, exploration and knowledge. They trim reality according to their needs and enforce their truth on every other iceberg. They do this by inducing fear in the other icebergs and, very astutely, they have a punishment for every wrong doing in their books. Anyone who dares to challenge their truth or criticize it receives punishment in the form of: imprisonment, numbing medication, persecution or death.

The strength of icebergs that live in this reality is their ability to twist information to their advantage. They are master liars and manipulators, masters of control. In this reality there is no freedom, only imprisonment, because every single iceberg that lives here is either at the top, enforcing their law and dogma, or terrified of moving outside that law or dogma, just in case the punishment threatened in the manuals is applied. The poison of greed and jealousy rots the icebergs in time, making them dull and easy to crack, even though they have advanced technology to fix everything and make it look shiny and new. When these icebergs are confronted they do not hesitate to strike hard to protect what they have lived for. Unfortunately, we can cite many examples from the experience of life in IRON reality:

...Mao Ze-Dong (China, 1958-61 and 1966-69, Tibet 1949-50) 49-78,000,000
Jozef Stalin (USSR, 1932-39) 23,000,000 (the purges plus Ukraine's famine)
Adolf Hitler (Germany, 1939-1945) 12,000,000 (concentration camps and civilians WWII)
Leopold II of Belgium (Congo, 1886-1908) 8,000,000
Hideki Tojo (Japan, 1941-44) 5,000,000 (civilians in WWII)
Ismail Enver (Turkey, 1915-20) 1,200,000 Armenians (1915) + 350,000 Greek Pontians and 480,000
Anatolian Greeks (1916-22) + 500,000 Assyrians (1915-20)
Pol Pot (Cambodia, 1975-79) 1,700,000
Kim Il Sung (North Korea, 1948-94) 1.6 million (purges and concentration camps)
Menghistu (Ethiopia, 1975-78) 1,500,000
Yakubu Gowon (Biafra, 1967-1970) 1,000,000
Leonid Brezhnev (Afghanistan, 1979-1982) 900,000
Jean Kambanda (Rwanda, 1994) 800,000
Suharto (East Timor, West Papua, Communists, 1966-98) 800,000
Saddam Hussein (Iran 1980-1990 and Kurdistan 1987-88) 600,000
Tito (Yugoslavia, 1945-1987) 570,000
Fumimaro Konoe (Japan, 1937-39) 500,000? (Chinese civilians)
Jonas Savimbi (Angola, 1975-2002) 400,000
Mullah Omar - Taliban (Afghanistan, 1986-2001) 400,000
Idi Amin (Uganda, 1969-1979) 300,000
Yahya Khan (Pakistan, 1970-71) 300,000 (Bangladesh)
Benito Mussolini (Ethiopia, 1936; Libya, 1934-45; Yugoslavia, WWII) 300,000
Mobutu Sese Seko (Zaire, 1965-97) ?
Charles Taylor (Liberia, 1989-1996) 220,000
Foday Sankoh (Sierra Leone, 1991-2000) 200,000
Michel Micombero (Burundi, 1972) 150,000
Slobodan Milosevic (Yugoslavia, 1992-99) 100,000
Hassan Turabi (Sudan, 1989-1999) 100,000
Jean-Bedel Bokassa (Centrafrica, 1966-79) ?
Richard Nixon (Vietnam, 1969-1974) 70,000 (Vietnamese and Cambodian civilians)
Efrain Rios Montt (Guatemala, 1982-83) 70,000
Papa Doc Duvalier (Haiti, 1957-71) 60,000
Hissene Habre (Chad, 1982-1990) 40,000
Chiang Kai-shek (Taiwan, 1947) 30,000 (popular uprising)
Vladimir Ilich Lenin (USSR, 1917-20) 30,000 (dissidents executed)
Francisco Franco (Spain) 30,000 (dissidents executed after the civil war)
Fidel Castro (Cuba, 1959-1999) 30,000
Lyndon Johnson (Vietnam, 1963-1968) 30,000
Hafez Al-Assad (Syria, 1980-2000) 25,000
Khomeini (Iran, 1979-89) 20,000
Robert Mugabe (Zimbabwe, 1982-87, Ndebele minority) 20,000
Rafael Videla (Argentina, 1976-83) 13,000
Guy Mollet (France, 1956-1957) 10,000 (war in Algeria)
Harold McMillans (Britain, 1952-56, Kenya's Mau-Mau rebellion) 10,000
Paul Koroma (Sierra Leone, 1997) 6,000
Osama Bin Laden (worldwide, 1993-2001) 3,500
Augusto Pinochet (Chile, 1973) 3,000
Al Zarqawi (Iraq, 2004-06)...

Around **187,000,000** icebergs were destroyed in genocides in the 20th century alone! This list does not include the non-official drug wars or mafia wars, or indeed the official and *'politically correct'* wars.

Those icebergs that have planned, orchestrated or supported Killing, Massacre, Famine or Genocide anywhere in the globe, have Fear, Anger, Depression, Jealousy, Desire and Greed running through their iceberg veins. Their ignorance is such that the afflictive emotions fully dictate their actions.

Although icebergs living in other realities are also challenged by these afflictive emotions, in the IRON reality these afflictive emotions are central to its shape and form. Unfortunately, this is the reality that we can all default to when we cannot deal consciously with Fear, Anger, Depression, Jealousy, Desire or Greed.

We have all at some point experienced one or more of these realities. The exploration of our iceberg and waters allows us to expand our understanding of what we are experiencing and of what we are living. We wake up from ignorance to a wider state of consciousness. We venture into the unknown by accident or by choice. We learn, we reflect and we expand our perspective of our own iceberg, other icebergs and the waters.

Ignorance at its strongest is when we lock ourselves into the position that claims: "All I see, or believe I see, is all there is to my iceberg, to other icebergs and to the water around the iceberg". This state of being is part of the IRON reality, where an individual perception creates a collective reality for all icebergs and the water itself. It is similar to the story of the colours when GREEN decided to alienate RED, or when GREY decided to ban COLOUR. We can see it at play all the time around the world when pharmaceutical companies test drugs with 'minorities'; when governments decide to invade other countries because they have what they want; when people that have been abused or molested are silenced with money; when people kill animals for entertainment and recreation.

The power of Ignorance can destroy, induce pain and create horror because we become unconscious puppets of the main afflictive states of consciousness:

Desire	Anger	Depression
Jealousy	Fear	Greed

When we are at the mercy of any of these states we have no control over our choices. The less conscious or awake we are, the more unconscious and Ignorant we become. These afflictive states are part of the waters that we live in and their essence runs through the information in the crystals of the iceberg. When most of who we are remains under water - unknown, unacknowledged and invisible to us – it is easier for these states to control and manipulate who we are.

The afflictive states serve as amplifiers of the information and the conditioning that resides within us, within the iceberg. Let's use the example of what happened to RED in chapter II in the example of the policeman interviewing three different suspects. Information was stored in the iceberg of the policeman that RED was evil, so fear came to dance with the policeman, amplifying his conditioning. Depending on his state of awareness, we could imagine two possible outcomes:

If the policeman is conscious about the fact that inside his iceberg is the belief that RED = evil then he will be very careful not to be biased towards RED. The policeman will know that he does not like RED and will try to be neutral and objective in spite of feeling afraid of RED.

However, if the policeman is unconscious to the fact that in his iceberg it was written that RED = evil, then when he is in the company of RED and when he hears RED speaking he will automatically block the information. The policeman will get a rush of uncomfortable feelings in his body when he is around RED and RED will then be convicted with no chance to defending its cause.

Ignorance is powerful. Who do you believe is more ignorant?

The mother that wants to fix her gay son
Or the son for being gay?

The bank employee for following orders and deceiving people
Or the 'Boss' for planning the scam?

The mother that agrees to give her children injections that can cause blindness because she needs money
Or the pharmaceutical company that creates the injections and the research in the first place?

The policeman that arrests a person as a murder suspect because he is homeless
Or the homeless for being homeless?

The person who fights to retrieve their home and country
Or the person who invaded the country and took their home and land away?

The girl that gets pregnant and keeps her child,
Or the girl that has an abortion?

What is gross ignorance and what is subtle ignorance? Who will be given the power to make the golden rule that will discern between what is allowed and what is not allowed?

Can you grasp the power that Ignorance has? It can make 'definite; things that are subjective to the individual perception of life. And it then creates judgement based on individual experiences and understanding of reality.

Ignorance is when we forget that we are the Light that reflects itself through water and shines, creating a beautiful RAINBOW. Ignorance is when we forget that we are a beautiful RAINBOW and choose to become a separate COLOUR. Ignorance is when we forget we are a COLOUR and we become GREY. Ignorance is when we believe in extremes, when we become too serious and radical. To live in Ignorance is to live in darkness, blind to other realities and adventures, believing that only what I see is real, true, and right.

Ignorance is the illness that creates separation and judgement, making unreal, false and wrong all that lies outside my personal window of vision.

When we experience ignorance in the IRON state we described before, we have a need to control and create a sense of who we are based on the external world. We need to fix and trim the information to fit our own perception and needs. While in the IRON state we have forgotten that we are part of the whole and we live at the mercy of the external reality and the world around us. We then need to feed on approval and power.

The subtle effects of Ignorance are harder to find because they remain under the deep waters of the unconscious. And as we experienced before, what is unconscious to me is not the same as what is unconscious to you. This is the information that is received by our senses and registered by our brain but, because of its weight, it sinks deep into the unconscious without us ever knowing it is there.

Once the information sinks below the surface, we live in the iceberg completely unaware of its existence, but permanently influenced by it. The territory we experience above the water in our conscious state is shaped by the territory that lies underneath the surface.

Icebergs are formed from frozen water. The ocean is made of water. When the water of the ocean starts lowering its temperature the water can then become a crystal. For us, the water crystallizes more with every single experience we have of separation. It separates from itself and it becomes solid, then it goes back into warm waters and melts. There are infinite possibilities to this cycle, but let's focus on one example. Every time the water crystallizes some of it does not melt again and then when it crystallizes again it starts adding on to itself, slowly forming a rock of ice; slowly growing; slowly becoming an iceberg. Every crystal of water is information, an experience of some kind. All the different crystals then make the totality of the iceberg.

These experiences accumulate to form the iceberg you have landed on:

BEFORE, DURING and AFTER
you opened your eyes and
found yourself sitting at the tip of the iceberg.

BEFORE, DURING and AFTER
you were conceived by your biological parents.

This means that before you ever existed, from the beginning of times, from the origin of the universe, from other oceans, from other planets, from every ancestor that became a separate individual or life form, all that happened encapsulates the crystals of experience BEFORE you were conceived. All that happened as you were dreamt into being - the shape of the crystals of your 'mother' and 'father', their biology and their thoughts, their emotions and their dreams, the act of conception in itself when you first became a crystal of water and gave life to the fecund egg - encapsulates the crystals of experience DURING conception. All that happened as the egg grew and became a foetus and all that followed - particularly during your entry into the world of icebergs, your own adventures and explorations of being an iceberg until you stop being an iceberg and die - encapsulates the crystals of experience AFTER conception.

All of this information forms the iceberg that you are now sitting and walking on. All this information, then, is what has given shape, form and size to your iceberg. No iceberg can be duplicated; all are unique and amazingly beautiful in their own right.

As we said before, this information lies deep inside the iceberg and deep under the water, so in the conscious state we are not usually aware, nor are we capable of perceiving the effects of all of this unconscious information.

After recognising that: "I am ignorant" then I have to recognise the existence of my conscious uncovered iceberg, which I can see, feel and touch, and the existence of my unconscious covered iceberg that I cannot see, feel or touch. I then have to acknowledge the existence of afflictive states that will amplify the information stored in my iceberg. So far I can say:

"I am ignorant, consciously and unconsciously,
dancing with desire, jealousy, anger, depression, fear and greed."

"...when trough all the doors of the body the light of body shines forth, it should be understood that there is an increase of Sattwa.

Greed, kinesis, initiative of action, unrest and craving of desire, these come forth, O Best of the Bharatas, when there is an increase of Rajas.

Obscurity, inertia, negligence and delusion, these come forth, O Joy of the Kurus, when there is an increase of Tamas.

If Sattwa prevails when the embodied soul meets with dissolution, then he attains the spotless worlds of the knowers of the Highest.

Meeting with dissolution when Rajas prevails, he is born among those attached to action; and if dissolved when Tamas prevails, he is born in the wombs of beings involved in nescience.

It is said that the fruit of works rightly done is pure and sattwic; grief is the fruit of rajasic and ignorance the fruit of tamasic works.

From Sattwa arises knowledge and from Rajas greed; from Tamas proceed negligence, delusion and also ignorance...."
(Bhagavad Gita)

Chapter IV
Is There Healing?

> "I am ignorant, consciously and unconsciously, dancing
> with desire, jealousy, anger, depression, fear and greed".

Is there healing for ignorance?
Yes, awareness of the ignorance.

Is there healing for unconsciousness?
Yes, consciousness of the unconsciousness.

Is there healing for the afflictive states of consciousness?
Yes, as you become conscious of the ignorance and unconsciousness
of desire then you can practice discernment and transmute desire;
for jealousy practice generosity; for anger practice compassion; for
depression practice detachment; for fear practice wisdom; and for
greed practice introspection.

The Story of Kamu the Clumsy Whale

*Deep in the ocean there once lived a clumsy whale named
Kamu. She was bigger than the other whales and her fins were
so large that she found it hard to keep control of them. She
would constantly knock things around and crash against other
whales making them really upset.*

*This particular morning the whales woke up to get ready for
their annual festival, where many of their sibling whales would
come to their waters and party. It was an ancient tradition from
the Whale tribe that no longer had much meaning but was still
practiced. They gathered and sang beautiful whale songs and
danced gracefully in deep waters. The climax of the festival
was always when the elder whales would teach the young
whales how to jump out of the water. All the whales would*

swim in circles around this beautiful display, proud of their young ones learning the tricks of being a whale. The young ones thought they knew how to jump without having the elders teach them in this ritual. Their participation was always reluctant and disdainful.

Kamu always felt alone and different and she would always step far away from this display because if she jumped her fins normally knocked down the little ones. She felt nothing for this ritual anymore. To her it was empty and had no soul.

The festival was on and after the singing and dancing the time came for the big jumping display. They all went to the surface and started the big show, water splashing. Kamu stayed away. She was getting tired of never being able to take part in the display and she couldn't stand the smell of hundreds of different perfumes on top of the beautiful natural smell of whale skin. This time she travelled a bit further away from the group. As she swam away she could hear the water splashing and the sound of the other whales pretending to have fun. They would have fun later when they indulge in Planktohol, a drink distilled from plankton, the perfect way to make them numb and forgetful.

She wondered and dreamed about a place where she could be accepted and where she could fit in. She dreamed of a place where whales would not forget and act stupid. As she swam further and further away she started feeling tired and went to sleep. When she woke up she didn't recognise where she was. She felt afraid and cried, blaming herself for leaving the tribe. She screamed and shouted but there was no sign of the other whales. She did not know what to do or where to go. She felt like dying and sank to the bottom of the sea in grief.

As her big body was sinking she felt something hitting against her and heard a scream:
"Hey you! Watch out!"
Who spoke? This was strange as she didn't know there was anyone else living in the ocean.

"Me! You big whale. I am Tiku the dolphin"

"Tiku? I didn't know dolphins could speak. I am Kamu the clumsy whale."

"I know who you are. I've heard about you. I've seen you. I know that you are never welcomed to the big jumping celebration because you knock everybody down."

"How come you know about me and I do not know about you?"

"Look Kamu, it was difficult for you to be so big and I understand that it was painful to be excluded and different but you took it all too seriously! The whales and the dolphins used to be friends. We used to talk and do things together but you never listened or noticed us around because you were too immersed in your own misery worrying about your clumsiness. But now whales love their planktohol too much and what used to be fun now ends up in arguments and rows, so we don't bother going there anymore."

"I know that but you were once there, weren't you? You must know Manik and Lara and the others?"

"Oh, Kamu. When are you going to learn? When are you going to wake up? Don't you know why you are clumsy?"

"Wait! Tiku if you say you know my tribe and where we live then you can take me back, can't you?"

"Kamu, you are not listening to me. I asked you if you know why you are clumsy?"

"Tiku don't mess with me. I don't care why I'm clumsy, I just want to get back! Come on let's not waste time!"

"I will take you back Kamu when you are prepared to listen."

"What! Are you mad? I knew I should never have spoken to you. I'm probably imagining all this, a dolphin talking? What nonsense!"

Tiku swam away leaving Kamu in her despair. Kamu swam in circles for days trying to find her way back. She wondered if her encounter with Tiku was real at all or if she had made it up. She thought she was going mad. She thought she was hearing voices and she sank deeper and deeper in the ocean of her misery. At the bottom she wished she could die so it would all go away. She believed then that the appearance of Tiku was a hallucination and that the tribe had a good reason not to want her around. After all, she was mad. Who would ever want to be around her?

Kamu got weak and she could no longer swim to get air. She fainted. But Tiku was never far away. Tiku called his tribe and between all the dolphins they pushed Kamu to the surface. They held her and sang for her until suddenly movement happened. Kamu was waking up! She took a big gasp of air and her whole body contorted in that breath. She opened her eyes again and saw the sun shining and felt the air on her skin!, Kamu swam and jumped with the happiness of being alive. When she stopped she saw Tiku and his tribe surrounding her and singing for her. She felt full of joy and for the first time she felt Love. Kamu cried of happiness and bliss.

"Tiku, I am sorry for not listening to you. In my dreams I saw my death and I saw my misery. I realised that my awkwardness consumed my life and I forgot completely that there was a world outside my big clumsy body. In my dreams I saw my tribe and all that I have missed because I was so absorbed in myself. In my dreams I saw you dancing with the whales and you spoke to me. You kept repeating "when you learn to listen I will take you back."
Tiku smiled. "Kamu are you willing to listen?"
"Yes, yes! Please Tiku tell me why I am clumsy!"
"First tell me why do you think you are clumsy?"
"Because I am too big and my fins too large?"
"Kamu how do you know you are too big and your fins too large?"
"Mmm, because they told me, because all the rest have smaller fins and are smaller than me."
"But clumsy has nothing to do with big or small Kamu. How do you know the other whales that are small are not clumsy?"
"Well, I do not know...wait the baby whales bump against the coral and the rocks and they get carried away by currents. That is clumsy too, isn't it?"
"So how come you separated from the tribe and the other clumsy whales didn't?"
"I do not know Tiku, I only know I did."

"Sleep on it. You must be tired. Take this purple alga, we use it to dream, this will help you to sleep and remember."

That night Kamu had a deep sleep and in her dreams she travelled far away to other oceans and to other worlds. In her dreams she travelled back in time and saw herself as a baby whale playing with the other baby whales. She saw her mother dancing with her and teaching her to sing the ancestral songs of the whale tribe. She felt joy and sadness, an overwhelming sadness as she experienced her early years. In the memories she did not see a clumsy big whale; she saw Kamu a beautiful and energetic baby whale. The dream continued like a movie for Kamu and she found herself at her first whale festival. She felt the excitement of her first jumping celebration and how she had been looking forward to this day since she was born.

The celebration started and she was to be the centre of attention that year because they never had a whale that had grown so big so fast with such spectacular and magnificent fins. From an early age she could swim faster than any other whale. She was strong and the pride of her tribe. Kamu witnessed the dream in awe, wondering how she could ever forget this.

But something went very wrong that year, something that was going to make Kamu forget.

As they made the circle and they sang their whale songs strange noises and waves approached; sounds they had never heard before, abrasive and pulsating; sounds that would disturb their capacity to hear. Boats, big boats and a strange tribe of animals in them; two-legged animals with long arms that ended in long metal claws. , They did not look friendly. In shock the whales tried to swim away but the boats followed them and forced them to swim towards the land. Whales knew the limits of their world and their ocean finished at edge of the land. They knew never to swim close to land because they could die. Some whales tried to separate from the herd with no success. The boats and the metal claws would strike against their bodies causing horrific pain, pain like they had never felt before. It was not the pain of the skin ripping open; it was the sting in their flesh of the anger and greed that came through the metal claws like poison. Fear, despair and panic took over the whale tribe. Kamu, being a magnificent whale, could swim faster than the others so she helped a few to break free and go deep under water to escape. But still some of the herd were taken to land and there was nothing they could do.

As the boats became distant they witnessed in their shock and tiredness the worst scene they could ever imagine.

The whales were taken to shore where the two-legged animals with metal claws came off the boats and began to strike the bodies of the whales, over and over, cutting them open, ripping the skin apart, the dying whales singing their song as they felt the pain and died in agony. The sea turned red, washing away the soul and the blood of her tribe.

Those who survived called for help and the dolphin tribe came. They realised that they could never swim in those waters again and so they swam far away, warning everyone on the way about the two-legged animals. Some believed them but others did not want to listen.

The Whale tribe found a new ocean and settled. Kamu did not speak for more than a year after what happened. She became a slow swimmer and her once magnificent fins became a big heavy burden. When Kamu spoke again she had apparently forgotten the events and the tribe thought it was for the best.

Kamu never felt full again, she carried herself with grief and an Emptiness that she could never explain.

Suddenly in the dream, she felt like flying and saw herself lifting from the water floating gently into the clouds. She went far beyond the clouds towards the sun. She felt the warmth and brightness of the beautiful yellow light. She then heard a song she had forgotten. The sound was like drops of ambrosia that filled her with love. She sang and as she sang the sun opened and she saw a rainbow ocean, bright and vast. In it she saw the elders of her tribe, singing to her. She felt indescribable peace as she approached them in the rainbow ocean. Kimpi, the oldest of the tribe, spoke to her: "Kamu it is time that you remember who you are. Do not grieve anymore. Make us proud and become all you were meant to be. Magnificent Kamu! Do not cry for us, we were never gone. We swim with you and we breathe with you. You must never feel alone. Do not be afraid, no bad can ever take hold of you, if you are true to your being. Your tribe are asleep and have worked hard to numb their pain. They have forgotten about the animals with metal claws. You must go back and help them remember. Take this with you. It is your soul and it will light the path when it's dark and it will keep your body warm. Welcome home Kamu."

Next morning, when Kamu woke up, she felt alive and tearful. She remembered clearly the dream as if it was real. She couldn't explain it but she knew inside that whatever happened in the dream was real and her sorrow was washed away.

"Good morning Kamu, how were your dreams?"
"Tiku I cannot really explain what happened but can you take me back? I have to go back to my tribe, they need me."
"Yes I will take you back. Do you think you could answer now why you thought you were clumsy?"
"Yes, I chose to forget who I was. I became a burden to myself. It was too painful. I could escape because I was big and fast, and those who were small died and I could not save them. I thought I did not deserve to be big and fast. Why me? Why not the others? I understand now that my greatness became my struggle. I went to sleep and I was afraid to wake up because I thought all that pain was going to wake up with me."
"And has the pain woken up after the dream?"
"Yes, I can feel the pain but I can see now what it is teaching me and how it is helping me remember who I am. I saw the tribe that died and I realised that they are not dead; they are alive in a rainbow ocean looking after me. I am not afraid anymore."
"I will take you back, but you must know that life will test you again and the darkness of the grief might call at your door. Learn to listen to it and do not be afraid of it."
"I will remember Tiku, I will remember."

Tiku and Kamu went swimming back to where the whale tribe lived. When they arrived the tribe could not contain their joy and they all gathered to welcome Kamu back. Kamu spoke to them about the past when they lived happily and about the massacre. She spoke about the Rainbow Ocean and Kimpi being alive in that ocean. They listened. The elders found strength and hope in the voices of their ancestors and started to sing the ancestral songs again, filling their hearts with joy and singing themselves back into their whale bodies.

The young ones learned the ancient ways of the whale tribe again and found that they had the capacity to sing. They found the true meaning of their festivals and celebrations that had been practiced as an empty routine. The whale tribe sang their song again and Kamu was made the leader of the tribe.

Some still did not listen and split from the tribe, swimming close to the waters of the two-legged animal with metal claws. They found death at their claws only then believing that the story was true. But while dying, as the yellow light appeared and the rainbow ocean shone, some were scared of the blinding light and travelled as far away from it as they could and others remembered Kamu's story and, although they were afraid, they travelled to the light.

Kamu swims now in the rainbow ocean with Kimpi singing the whale ancestral songs that help other whales to remember and find their way into the rainbow again.

In our evolution towards enlightenment or freedom from suffering, we will pass through many different states of awareness. We spoke in a simplistic manner about the COTTON reality, the PAPER reality, the IRON reality, etc... As we evolve through these states of consciousness we become more aware and more conscious about ourselves. But this awareness does not mean that Ignorance and unconsciousness disappear and vanish.

These two qualities of life remain with us until we reach transcendence of the separate state as a human being, when we attain enlightenment or absolute 'selflessness'. The myth that we like to believe in the western world is that once we open up to a spiritual path or read self-help or spiritual books these two qualities dissipate and evaporate from our being. But they don't because they are natural attributes of human existence.

When we claim to have reached realisation or liberation because of our academic efforts, without having explored any aspect of our own iceberg, we are living in denial and we described this state before as the IRON state of awareness in which the person believes: "I have 'arrived' and I have no need to look at myself anymore because all has been processed, all has been prayed away, or all has been sorted out in therapy or replaced with positive thinking."

This is a very dangerous state because when power and authority meet this level of ignorance, they influence the many icebergs that are committed or subdued to their authority. The higher our qualifications as psychiatrist, medical doctor, scientist, lawyer, counsellor, healer or priest, the more we are likely to believe that:

"What I see and what I believe are all that is relevant to my iceberg, other icebergs and the water around the iceberg"

Then we are living from an IRON state of awareness, powerfully blind.

Perhaps I believe that the best answer to life is:

~ Psychoanalysis because I am Freudian,
~ Medication because I am a biological Doctor,
~ Mass because I am a Priest,
~ Drumming because I am a Healer.....

Then we are acting in the same manner as GREEN did when it woke up and felt very GREEN and decided to alienate RED because it was a threat to its GREENness. In that moment we have forgotten that we are from the RAINBOW people, from the LIGHT and not separate and omnipotent GREEN, having all the answers for the rest of the COLOUR people. If you remember the story about the RAINBOW people this attitude is what made them ban colour from life and the world then became GREY. One truth for all, GREYNESS, and the true nature of the COLOUR people was washed away.

The healing for ignorance is the acknowledgement of ignorance. When I know I am ignorant because I have a limited perspective of the universe and reality when I sit on an iceberg, I become free. It is then that the afflictive emotions can become conscious and become apparent to the conscious mind. Only when these emotions are visible can I transmute them to their polar opposites. I don't get rid of them, I must transmute them.

When I sit in consciousness and awareness that desire; discernment, jealousy; generosity, anger; compassion, depression; detachment, fear; wisdom and greed; introspection, are all going to come and dance with me at different times, then what is there to fear?

If I sit in awareness of my ignorance and unconsciousness, then there is no need to be right or wrong. I sit and contemplate who I am in understanding and compassion of my ignorance and blindness. If I trip because I am blind I do not judge myself, blame myself or feel shame towards myself. I feel compassion, love and understanding because I am blind. Do you laugh at somebody who is blind and trips on the ground? Most people don't. In fact they will run to help and guide the blind person in the right direction with kindness and love. So why should I treat my blindness any different and laugh and criticise myself when I trip or stumble?

Sometimes it is easier to feel compassion for another person or being because we can visibly see their struggle, pain or blindness. It is commendable to have awareness and empathy towards other people's story. But how is it then so hard sometimes to reflect that same compassion and kindness towards ourselves?

We are at present experiencing a life where COLOUR has been banned and where the IRON state of awareness is predominant. In this world we have been born believing that reality is what we see outside ourselves and nothing more. We are living like the whale tribe at the beginning of Kamu's story where the community was part of meaningless rituals, the young thought they knew better than the elders and the highlight of life was Planktohol.

The inner reality, the COLOURness and RAINBOWness have been left in the iceberg that lies underneath the water, unconscious to our conscious life. We have become numb and blind to the rest of the iceberg that lies underneath the water. We are living life as if all there is to it is tips of icebergs. We engage, communicate and dance at the surface level, only seeing from each other and the world tips of icebergs. Anyone suggesting there is more to that reality is considered eccentric or, if unlucky, they are numbed and locked away. Today we laugh and have become cynical of COLOURnes and RAINBOWness. We are arrogantly content and numb in our GREYness.

When we first open up to COLOURness and RAINBOWness we relate to it at the surface level, still only at the tip of the iceberg and we apply our new understanding only to what we see over the surface. We become tolerant and empathic towards small icebergs, broken icebergs, fat icebergs, and so on. At this level of awareness we can help each other and support each other in our conscious struggle to find meaning as a tip of an iceberg, but the big 'elephant in the room' remains unseen and unmentioned - the whole of the iceberg!

When we live only on the surface things get fixed, icebergs get repaired. Let's say that I have a great capacity to repair icebergs. I am skilled with my hands and I have talent and vision like no other iceberg. Icebergs come to me and ask to be repaired because they are broken or cracked. I look at the iceberg, I clearly see the fault, and I proceed to add water to it and freeze it at a slow pace so I can give it shape...and surprise! Iceberg fixed! It looks beautiful and whole to me; it looks just like my mother used to look like, what a coincidence!

No matter how skilled I am as an iceberg repairer I will always repair what is broken according to my unconscious desires and impulses.

The information that lies in the rest of my iceberg will influence what I see and how I see it. If then I am allowed to repair the whole of iceberg town, in a very short time all Icebergs will look all the same, just like my mother!

When we acknowledge that under the surface there is a vast iceberg and an infinite ocean where the icebergs are born and die into, our perception of life changes radically. All of a sudden the tip of the iceberg becomes what it is - only the top and visible part of a whole iceberg. My vision expands to understand that as long as I live on the surface above the water a lot of the iceberg will remain unseen and not experienced and therefore I will live in ignorance of the totality of what is around me. I will then understand that, although I can learn to observe and acknowledge the iceberg underneath me, and although I can learn to swim into deep waters, I am still a tip of an iceberg, and when I come back to the surface, part of the iceberg will still remain covered by water, becoming unconscious to me and the water will remain as water - endless, infinite and eternal.

How can I master my unconsciousness? I can become the master of my own iceberg by acknowledging that it is there, by acknowledging that it is unconscious. The unconscious mind cannot be switched off; it is always active and running. Denying that there is a whole iceberg submerged in water under the tip I am sitting on will not make it disappear. Our unconscious is constantly informing our, emotions, our, thoughts and our actions. When we deny its presence, it becomes more powerful and we become puppets of the conditioning that is written in each one of its water crystals.

When we know it is there we understand that thoughts, feelings and behaviours will float to the surface unexpectedly and illogically. This happens because the conscious mind can't see the information that has been triggered underneath the water. All we see is what emerges to the surface and most of the time it does not directly correspond to our conscious experience. This makes us feel that there is a discrepancy or conflict in what we are feeling and we proceed to dismiss the information.

In order to acknowledge our ignorance of unconsciousness and afflictive emotions we need to explore the territory of attachment and detachment. We can look at these in the story of Kamu, the clumsy whale.

The whale tribe was awake and living consciously until one day a painful experience occurred. Another tribe, the two-legged tribe in their own ignorance found pleasure and excitement in slaughtering whales. After that painful experience Kamu went silent and eventually forgot what happened. Her once magnificent fins and size became a burden that made her clumsy. She believed that she was clumsy and she did not see any privilege or advantage in being big or having large fins. Kamu became attached to the idea that her fins and size made her clumsy and that became her only reality. Her attachment drove her into depression and isolation; it separated Kamu from her tribe.

Just like Kamu we become over-identified with who we think we are, with what we feel we are and with what we see we are. We allow our GREYness to become all we know about ourselves and all we ever want to know about ourselves. In that moment we are attached. With attachment immediately comes fear. I know I am a clumsy whale and all outside that concept becomes strange, unknown and different. When I am attached to something I fear losing it because I am attached, because it is my unique reality and I do not know how to live without it. From attachment and fear then arises suffering.

When I think all I am is GREY and I believe GREY to be the only one true reality to myself and to life then I am attached to my GREYness. I am automatically fearful of anything that challenges my GREYness and I become defensive and protective of GREY. When somebody comes and tells me that YELLOW exists I feel afraid and I suffer because it means that GREY then is not the only one absolute truth. It means that as there is GREY there is YELLOW and my whole experience of life and the world shakes and stumbles.

What causes me to suffer is not my ignorance regarding the existence of YELLOW but my attachment to GREY as the absolute reality. Suffering comes from attachment and attachment comes from Ignorance. Fear becomes the glue that holds these three concepts together.

For Kamu, GREY meant being clumsy, what does GREY mean to you?

Is GREY your job; your partner; your religion; your car; your children? Is it your country; money; clothes; life; science; make-up; anxiety; food; peace; depression; happiness; remaining young forever; anger; fame; approval; love; power...?

The list is infinite, as possibilities are infinite in the universe of experiencing life and living. The list is as vast as there are icebergs of infinite beauty and majesty, always unique in their being, always with individual qualities and general qualities. These words that we use to describe who we are form the tip of the iceberg. They are the symptoms of the illness, and they are your personal:

"I AMness"

Attachment makes us want to control reality in a way that our GREYness can always be there as the only one truth, always alive, always permanent, never changing. My ignorance then allows me to attach to something and because I am afraid of losing it, I wish to defend and protect it, making it permanent. My life then becomes a quest to maintain permanence and make my GREYness perpetual.
This continuous effort to make my life permanent becomes a real struggle when we are trying to do it in a world that in its entire essence is:

IMPERMANENT

How powerfully blinding is the illness we carry that tells us that, although all that surrounds us is impermanent, our life purpose is to flow against nature trying to stop the world and make it permanent!

If we were to look at the way we live from outside the Earth, we would see a fly trying to stop the Earth from spinning! Someone out there, if there is anybody out there, must be having a big, warm belly laugh watching us!

We suffer to the extent that we are attached. I am attached to my GREYness, I fear losing it, so in trying to make my GREYness permanent, I suffer because it is impossible. Then when I inevitably lose my GREYness, I suffer because I do not have it anymore and I live attached to the times when I had it. In this way I never live in the present moment because I am either trying to protect GREY or I'm grieving GREY.

I spend my life trying to protect my fame as a musician. Then when it is gone I live grieving its loss or trying to get it back. I live my life trying to protect my children and then when they are gone, I live grieving that they are gone or trying to get them back. I live my life trying to protect my beliefs and when they are gone I live grieving their loss and trying to get them back.

The scandalous aspect of Ignorance and attachment is when we realise that we go through this process with everything, big things and small things. When the shop keeper does not have what you want; when your partner does not perform as you want; when someone scratches your new car; when the maid shrinks your clothes; you when you don't get the present you want; when the nightclub does not play music you like; when your skin tan fades away; the wind blows and your hair gets disrupted; when the boyfriend does not call; when your child gets a bad mark at school; when the waiter is too slow; every single time you don't get what you want exactly as you want it!

Some situations like terminal illness, murder, abuse or grief are extremely serious and we believe justifiable of suffering. And from a human perspective they are horrifying realities - hard, if not impossible to digest. Nevertheless, the process of attachment applies to them in the same manner as to everything else because **suffering and pain are different realities**. All these experiences are excruciatingly painful for us, but we only suffer with them when we over-identify with them; when we attach to them; when we forget that as much as you are human, you are also more than that.

In Kamu's story after the painful experience of losing her tribe to the metal claws of the two-legged animals Kamu attached to the pain and suffered immensely. But then one day she realised that a rainbow ocean existed and that her tribe had always been beside her. She remembered, and after her dream she suffered no more. **She could feel the pain of the experience but she was no longer suffering.**

Kamu freed herself from fear when she almost died and Tiku and his tribe helped her to rise above the water again coming back to life. In that moment, Kamu, dissolved her fear. As the fear dissolved so did the attachment to her misery. Remember that fear is the glue that holds together ignorance, attachment and suffering. In that moment she wanted to know more, she was willing to listen to Tiku, she no longer wished to be ignorant and she woke up from her sleep.

Awareness does not wash away the pain of losing a child or having cancer, or having your land stolen by GREEN people, but it frees you from suffering from it. You will still have to bare the pain of being human, but your heart will be at peace and your attention will be in the present moment, even if you feel that burning pain inside you for a time.

Many times in life we choose to forget because we feel the burning pain of life, and we anaesthetise ourselves with substances, business or denial. In that chosen ignorance we can be blissfully happy. It is a way of numbing the pain of life circumstances, but it's not a magic wand, and the life circumstances and the pain does not go away because we choose to deny it. They will be there walking side by side with you as you live, right in front of you when you die and going with you when you live again.

If it is fear that keeps ignorance, attachment and suffering together, what is it that we are so afraid of?

We could name many different things we are afraid of. Every one of us has personal experiences that help us attach fear to the devil, to the bogey man, to insects, to frogs, to rats, to worms, to ill heath, to flowers, to feathers, to darkness, to airplanes, and so on.

What we attach the fear to is not the cause or source of fear; it is simply a piece of the puzzle of who we are. What we attach the fear to gives us a metaphorical or literal idea of the information that is stored in the water crystals of the iceberg underneath the water, the unconscious iceberg. It can help us to understand the iceberg but it is not the source of the fear, it is simple a reflection of the fear. It is a way in which we can look at the fear as a mirror. I am afraid I cannot see the fear until I attach it to something, so in the moment I attach it to RED, COLOUR, GREY, then I can see the fear.

The source of the fear in our realm of human existence is related to our experience of permanence and impermanence. When we live in a human body and experience ignorance and attachment we crave ignorance for permanence. As the world around us is impermanent the ignorant desire for permanence feeds the fear of impermanence. We become afraid of change and transformation. We become afraid of dying. Ultimately what we fear is:

DEATH

Is there healing for ignorance?
Yes.

Is there healing for unconsciousness?
Yes.

Is there healing for the afflictive states of consciousness?
Yes.

Is there healing for the fear of Death?
Yes, Die. Die to the idea of who you are.

*"...They are encircled by two male bodhisattvas,
Ākāśagarbha and Samantabhadra, and two
female bodhisattvas, Mālyā and Dhūpā, thus six
buddha-bodies will be shining before you from
within a space of rainbow light.*

*A yellow light [indicative of] the pristine cognition
of sameness, which is the natural purity of the
aggregate of feeling, yellow and dazzling,
adorned by greater and lesser seminal points [of
light], radiant clear and unbearable to the eyes,
[will emanate] from the heart of Ratnasambhava
and his consort and will shine piercingly before
you at the level of your heart [with such
brilliance] that your eyes cannot bear it.
Together with the light of pristine cognition, a
blue dull light, [indicative of] the human realm,
will also dawn before you and touch your heart.
At that time under the sway of pride, you will
[wish to] turn away in fear and terror from the
bright yellow light and you will come to delight in
the dull blue light of the human realm and feel
attachment towards it. At that moment,
abandon your fear of the yellow light, and
recognize it as pristine cognition, yellow and
dazzling, radiant and clear! Let your awareness
relax and abide directly within it, in a state of
non-activity. Again and again, have confidence
in it! Be drawn to it with longing devotion! If you
recognize it as the natural luminosity of your own
awareness, even though you may feel no
devotion towards it and have not recited the
aspirational prayer, all the buddha-bodies and
light rays will dissolve inseparably into you and
you will attain buddhahood..."*
(Tibetan Book of the Dead)

Section Two
Lost Sovereignty

"I am free only when I realise I am sovereign;
I am sovereign only when I empty myself of fear;
I empty myself of fear when I learn to die"
Ná Áak

Chapter V
Forgotten Voices

The story of the Creation of Tule

The Earth was a quiet and harmonious place where a beautiful symphony of sacred whispers could be admired and enjoyed at all times. Different tunes and different sounds would play according to the seasons of the Earth.

Standing tall and wide on the surface of the Earth was Tule, the magnificent. Tule was a tree, as ancient as the mountains and as profound and deep as the oceans. He stood witnessing all that surrounded him. Every day Tule sang with the wind and spoke to the soil around its roots. He played with the clouds and laughed with the rain. But what Tule loved the most was to witness the beautiful dance that happened in the sky as brightness and darkness preceded and accompanied each other. This was the cosmic dance of two well-known characters Ometecutli and Omecihuatl. They were known as the sacred couple of feathered-dragons that animated and gave birth to all that has material form.

The dance usually commenced at the crack of dawn, as the first ray of light would shine showing Ometecutli as ball of fire. As the brightness of this fire, the Sun, emerged, both dragons would melt into each other, transforming the sky into a breathtaking display of rainbow colours. As the dance would unfold, more and more brightness would engulf the night sky, gently and slowly, the Sun caressing darkness; only to completely swallow it in her radiance.

The Sun would shine bright and tall warming the Earth with Tule bringing them into life. At sunset, when it was time for the Sun to shine in another horizon, she would pull her veil of brightness, revealing slowly and gently the face of her beloved consort, Omecihuatl the Moon. The feathered-dragons would lose themselves in a passionate dance exploding into rainbow light, making Tule cry. As the Sun went down in the horizon, the darkness of the night would engulf the Earth and Tule, bringing silence, calmness and rest.

Tule was privileged to witness this display every day and every night, welcoming the beauty of brightness and darkness. He could never imagine a world without the fire of the sun and the calmness of the moon.

One day Tule wondered about his origins and started to feel the need to understand more about the dance that he was witnessing in the sky, the dance that made day and night and the dance that made other plants and trees lose their leaves and then grow them back.

Tule always felt there was something wrong with him because his branches were never naked of leaves, like the other trees were. "How come I am different?" Tule wondered. "Maybe there is something missing in me, or maybe I have too much of something." As the days and the seasons went by, Tule found himself immersed more and more in confusion and turmoil until one day he could no longer see the beauty in the dance of dawn and dusk. Tule was depressed.

The wind noticed Tule's distress and called an emergency meeting with all the other elements and directions. Sitting on a cloud, the Sun, the Moon, Water, Ether, East, West, North, South, the Earth and Wind assessed Tule's situation.
The consensus was unanimous, "It is time to show Tule the truth, he is ready."

The next morning after dawn, Wind, always the carrier of news, approached Tule:
"Good morning Tule, are you ready for an exciting day?"
"Hello Wind, and why is it an exciting day? Is today the day when the other trees lose their leaves, or when the daffodils come out? I can't remember."

"I mean an exciting day for you, Tule."

"What can be exciting for me? I stand here always in the same spot, doing the same thing, never moving never changing; only getting taller and wider."

"There are many things, Tule, that you do not know about life and this Earth and we feel it is time for you to remember who you are."

"Who's we? Remember who I am? I am Tule! the tree that never loses its leaves and only increases in size. While all the others seem to enjoy seasons, I stand here alone and unchanged."

"Tule, you are confused and I understand why you see life in that way. But if you let me, I can show you something that will change you forever."

"Are you going to make my leaves fall? Because you'll have to blow very hard, Wind, for that to happen."

"I won't make your leaves fall, Tule. I would be taking away who you are, if I do that."

"Well who I am is a curse and I wish I was like the others."

"If you let me I can show you the reason why you are like this."

"Would that change anything?"

"It might, or it might not, but at least you will know then."

"Ok Wind, I suppose I have nothing to lose, show me."

"Just close your eyes Tule and follow my voice. All you need to do is breathe with me Tule, just let me rock you and breathe with me gently."

Tule hesitantly closed his eyes and started to feel the pulse of the Wind, back and forth, back and forth. Tule felt embraced and rocked with the gentle wind. "Breathe Tule, breathe with me." The Wind started to move faster and stronger and for a moment Tule felt afraid. He thought he was going to break, but for some strange reason he felt safe and it remembered "I have nothing to lose." As the wind gained strength and power, Tule felt his roots lifting from the soil and felt light as if he could fly. "Breathe Tule, breathe with me." Suddenly Tule opened his eyes and looked down. to see that he was levitating above the Earth! He felt sick. "Breathe Tule, breathe with me". As Tule breathed with the Wind he became violently ill, letting go of heavy darkness and vile. He felt relief! And like magic he *became lighter and started to ascend upwards and upwards through the tornado that Wind was breathing for Tule. "Breathe Tule, breathe."*

Tule felt lifted into to the sky and when he looked down he could see the Earth where he once stood tall, and the Wind breathing for him pushing him further and further into the sky until he rose above the atmosphere of the Earth.

Floating in space Tule experienced silence and his eyes witnessed the beauty of the Sun and the Earth, and it saw that there were other planets. When he looked over his trunk he saw a silver string coming out of his 'middle'. This string was pulling him somewhere, and he had no idea what that string was or where he was going but he had never felt so much peace. He let it be.

It seemed he was being pulled into colour clouds and tingling dust, but as he went further he saw in the distance big mountains! This was strange in the middle of nothingness and cosmic dust, mountains? "Where is this? What is this?" he asked.

A radiant rainbow light was shining from behind the mountains and he felt an overwhelming sense of space inside his trunk, air that was not air, warm, serene and gentle love. "Home! I am home!" he thought.

As he came close to the peak of the mountains he could not believe what he witnessed: more vibrant colours than had ever been painted, gentler sounds than had ever been sung, more magnificent shapes than had ever been sculpted, sweeter tastes than had ever been poured.

Now he saw where the silver string was coming from. In the valley between the mountains there was a lake full of lotus flowers shining beautifully and sitting peacefully on the water. Each flower had a shape, a being sitting on it. His string was coming from the song that one of the figures on the lotus was singing. It was as if Tule's song was being sung by this creature and the sound itself created the string.

Once Tule descended to firm land, the being on the flower came to meet him.
"Namaste Tule."
"...where am I?"
"You are home."
"Did you bring me here?"
"No Tule, you brought yourself here. I just sang so you would not get lost. What do you want Tule?"
"I don't know, I...I was breathing with Wind and then...I don't know."
"Don't try so hard. Just tell me, what do you feel inside?"
"I feel full now, whole! Yes I feel Whole!"
"If you can feel the wholeness now it means that you once felt empty."
"That is it! I was on Earth and I was this big tree, and I was standing there seeing all other trees change leaves and flowers and I never changed. I keep getting wider and I don't want to be different, I want to be like the other trees. But Wind came and told me he was going to help me remember who I was."
"So maybe that is why you came here, to remember."
"Maybe, yes, maybe, no, yes!, I don't know."
"Relax Tule, would it help if I tell you a story?"
"Yes, please."
"Let's sit and close your eyes. Listen to my voice and try to imagine what you hear:"

Once upon a time there was a Universe made of pure ambrosia; nectar that permeated through all things keeping them always connected, holding together the whole Universe. This nectar was a soft white fluid, warm and sweet, always present and eternally pouring. This nectar responded to the sound of it its name, Ometeotl.

Ometeotl was the One; essence of all that could possibly be created; it was an ocean of infinite possibilities of manifestation, the substance that made creation possible.

It was known that before Ometeotl, there was nothing, only Emptiness and absolute silence. No form, no sound, no light, only empty space. Emptiness was known as the in-between space, the pause before the Universal Outbreath and the Universal Inbreath. Emptiness was the place for Ometeotl to rest after its magnificent adventures. The entire Universe knew that the only possible way to arrive at Emptiness and rest was to be taken by Catrina [the lady of Death], the giver of rest, the bridge between breaths, the weaver of the Universal Inbreath and the Universal Outbreath. It was Catrina, [Death] who guided all that ever existed into its resting place, into Emptiness, including Ometeotl. And she accompanied all that would want to be created into life.

Catrina knew every corner of the Universe and travelled from Emptiness to the confinement of the Universal Outbreath of creation, weaving it in to the Universal Inbreath and so into Emptiness again.

This weaving back and forth, facilitated by Catrina, was known as the pulse of life: Prana. This natural and harmonious rhythm gave the Universe its impermanent nature, because its very existence was to be always flowing, always changing, always moving, always breathing, always evolving and always dying. This pulse was known to be eternal.

All in the Universe were grateful and generous towards Catrina because it was thanks to her that they all could rest and that the Universe had a pulse. Without her weaving Inbreath, Outbreath and Emptiness their Universe would simply have never existed and Prana would have never taken its first breath. Catrina was the pacemaker of the Heart of the Universe.

This Heart of the Universe was located somewhere to the east of the sacred mountain of Kailas. The Heart place, commonly known by the name of Paititi, was a place of immense beauty, rainbow light and peacefulness. Paititi was full of rainbow lakes that were filled with white lotus flowers. In here was where the

White Lotus, the observer of the Universe, sat in contemplation, awe, compassion and unconditional love of creation.

In Paititi only crystal clear awareness reigned, and this diamond-like awareness was translucid, permitting the golden light to shine through it. ; this will be the reason Tule, why many, in times to come, will set on utopian expeditions searching for a city made of pure gold; without realizing that it is golden because its translucent nature allows the light to shine through it.

White Lotus was able to witness all Emptiness be empty, all Outbreath breathe out, and all Inbreath breathe in. The White Lotus did not dance with the pulse of Catrina [Death] because it occupied the seat at the centre of the dance; it was the eternal, omnipresent and pure eye of crystal clear wisdom.

White Lotus sat at the lakes of Paititi together with thousands of White Lotuses inwards and outwards of its belly. As many White Lotuses as ones vision could perceive.

Every time that Catrina was called, as the midwife, to give birth to Universes, she was sung out of the belly of White Lotus through a silver string. At this moment a ray of Light would explode in tremendous heat making a big, big bang noise. The Light would then transform into a display of breathtaking rainbow light colours expanding fast and far, as far as it could be perceived. This big, bang was known as the Outbreath of the Universe.

The explosion of colours and light could only be perceived because the canvas in which it exploded was a mantel of dark emptiness. It was said that once the Universe learned to breathe, the Universe became a place of a thousand Outbreaths that shone from the distance like stars of rainbow colours hanging from the darkness.

As the rainbow light would slow and cool down then Ometeotl, the sweet nectar, could be differentiated. This transformation of form from light into nectar was the doing of Catrina as well, helping the Universe to morph into infinite shapes without any drop of light ever being lost or wasted.

Ometeotl, now born, would pour itself, expanding and creating an infinite ocean of ambrosia, an ocean of Quanta; Ometeotl! The quantum soup.

From Ometeotl's soup, two forces would emerge, the mirror images of light and darkness. Two feathered-dragons, named Ometecutli and Omecihuatl. These feathered-dragons were consorts, lovers; the sacred couple complementing each other to perfection. They were powerful and fearsome, passionate and loving, kind and ruthless. Each one of them carried an opposite essence and nature. Ometecutli was, in essence, loud, bright and active; it was yang. Omecihuatl was, in essence quiet, dark and restful; it was ying.

The code of life was carried by Ometeotl, Ometecutli and Omecihuatl in their very essence, encrypted in a manner that only those who knew how to count could decipher. The code of life contained all of the information that Ometeotl carried in its Akashic memory which was formed by all its previous and forthcoming adventures. Remember this Tule, this code lies always visible and readable in all manifestations of creation including you.

"Can you picture the story Tule?"
"Yes! It's so simple and complex at the same time, I recognize the dragons I remember seeing them dancing at dawn and dusk, only I did not know their names."
"Do not open your eyes. Can you see the dragons right now?"
"Yes I am standing in front of them. They are looking back at me. I can feel their power and heat rushing through my trunk."
"Good. Now, right where you are close your eyes and go inside again!"
"Oh I feel I am falling!"
"That is good. Fall Tule, let yourself free fall. Now tell me what do you see...?"

A Universe full of Light and Sound
"Emptiness! The code starts in Emptiness!. The absence of existence which corresponds to zero (0), no count no value. In zero White Lotus rests responding to the count of one (1). Creation does not replace itself but rather emerges from one another. The one who understands this can then understand that Emptiness, zero (0) and White Lotus, one (1) gave birth to Ometeotl, who counts one (1)."

"Good Tule, just continue downloading..."

A universe full of gas and matter
"The one who follows creation in awe and contemplation can easily piece together the next equation; White Lotus (1) and Ometeotl (1) gave birth to the feathered-dragons, Ometecutli and Omecihuatl counting two (2). Always unfolding and expanding according to the sacred count I now see emerging the sacred Trinity (3), it is born from the natural union of Ometeotl (1) and the sacred feathered-dragons (2).

The one who has Crystal clear awareness understands that the trinity is only a trinity because of the sacred union of one and two, Ometeotl and its consorts; the one essence of life and its dual manifestation as 'the mother' and 'the father' of all of creation. This is the eternal paradox that will permeate all forms that follow. This is the 'key-note' for harmonious creation.

Dissonant and disharmonious creation will emerge if any of this, in ignorance, becomes denied and forgotten. As Ometecutli and Omecihuatl cannot exist separate from Ometeotl, so the trinity (3) cannot exist separate from its essential nature; union (1) and separation (2); pure being and phenomena.

As a result of these manifestations the Universe is filling with thousands of Earths and Moons, spinning around thousands of Suns, dancing in dawn and dusk, shining their light in the canvas of darkness.

Some of these Earths are so precisely located in the Universe that they become a perfect place for Yemaya the lady of the waters, to pour herself from the gases in the sky into deep and rich oceans. That is how these lifeless masses of condensed matter became sustainable wombs that could cradle life. Yemaya made them fertile!"

"Keep going Tule..."

A Universe full of organic life
"The next step of the dance of creation implies a challenge. More complex form and life is to unfold from Ometeotl's quantum soup. The sacred feathered-dragons (2) have to dance with the threefold sacred union (3). Out of this dance a miracle is born!

Tule's eyes poured with tears...

"Lucia Aminoacida (5), organic life!
Yemaya kindly offers her waters in the thousands of oceans and in the thousands of Earths for Lucia to be born. The thousands of Suns offer their light and heat to warm the waters of Yemaya and help Lucia to grow and evolve."

A universe of sentient and intellectual life
"The sacred union formed by, Ometeotl and its consorts (3) cannot help to fall deeply in love with Lucia Aminoacida (5). She moves so graciously in the water that she can put anyone into a trance. Ometeotl and the feathered-dragons could not resist her enigmatic and sensual moves and after a few charms, Ooooh! The three fold union melted with Lucia Aminoacida giving birth to a more complex miracle! What is this? DaNA (8)!

DaNA, precious child of the Omecihuatl and Ometecutli, you are a small version of the feathered-dragons, twisted into yourself, carrying Light, carrying Darkness, carrying the code of life!"

"Tule, where are you now?"

"I am looking at DaNA swimming in the ocean, she is so beautiful. Wait she is calling me, I am leaning at the shore of the ocean."

"Dive Tule, let her show you, close your eyes and dive deep..."

"This ocean is big.........ooooooh....... I am DaNA! it is me! I have become DaNA!"

"Good Tule. Be DaNA and swim deep..."

The birth of DaNA

"I am swimming in the ocean. I feel good. All is contained and warm. I feel like I do in the mountains, whole and at peace. I didn't know that the waters of Yemaya were so sweet.
(A strong tide moved the waters)

What was that!? I felt a tremor, wait! There it is again. The waters are moving. I think I heard the soil crack as if the ocean has indigestion!?

Oh good! It is gone now.

Ooops! There it is again?! Yemaya! What is happening?! Are you ok?"

A big roar emerged from the depths of Yemaya making all the waters turbulent and dangerous.

"I am scared! Yemaya! What is happening?!
Wait! I do not want to play anymore, I don't want to be DaNA This is scary, I want to go back!! You Lotus, where are you now that I need you?! Take me out of here! This is not funny!"

The waters became more and more difficult to swim in and an earthquake cracked the bottom of the ocean, releasing strange gases making the water go bitter. From the crack a huge monster was unleashed. The monster travelled fast through the waters, devouring anything that crossed its path. The monster was like an enormous snake, only it had fins like a sea-dragon and teeth like a shark.

"What is that?! It is devouring everything! I'd better swim fast! Look, a red coral reef! Maybe if I hide there the monster will not find me."

What Tule did not know was that the monster was simply Catrina dressed in the suit of a sea dragon coming to serve as midwife for Tule to be born. When Catrina has a mission she completes it with no hesitation. That is how she cornered Tule between the red coral reef and the bottom of the ocean. Tule awaited his defeat in terror.

The monster would not rest and kept pushing until it started cracking the coral that was protecting Tule.

"Where are you?! Take me out of here! I am going to die!?"

When no answer came, Tule gave up. In that very instant another earthquake opened a big crack exactly under the coral where Tule was hiding, making Tule's head slip through the crack. In terror and trapped in the crack, Tule felt rage for having been abandoned and decided to fight for its life.

Tule started crawling through the crack. It was tight and pitch dark but he was determined, he was going to live!
Finally, at the other end, Tule could see some light. He felt afraid, but having gone so far into the crack there was no going back now. Tule felt he would probably die of tiredness and suffocation as he choked with the waters coming through the crack as well. But he kept on going and finally his head came out the other side of the crack, air! Tule could breathe!

In that moment Tule heard inside him the voice of the wind "Breathe Tule, breathe with me." Inspired by the voice and in a last attempt to survive Tule roared and pushed really hard. At the same time it heard Yemaya screaming in agony as one last earthquake pushed Tule outside the crack.

Tule felt cold and exposed. He cried. But suddenly when Tule opened his eyes he realised he had just popped out from the soil. A small, weak trunk, with one leaf on one flimsy branch. Tule looked around and in the distance saw the ocean, Yemaya, smiling proud at him. Tule looked up and felt blinded by the radiance and warmth of the Sun, waving her long arms at the newly born Tule. Around it only empty Earth, Tule the very first tree.

"Tule where are you now?"

"I am here. I am baby Tule. Where were you Lotus?!"

"I was always here, but your fear made you deaf to the sound of my voice. Still I sang your song so you would not get lost, and I can see you didn't."

"What now? Do I have to grow again?"

"No Tule, you are still asleep. Just open your eyes."

"Listen to me Lotus, I am tired of your wise sayings, I have my eyes open! Just get me out of here!"

Lotus smiled. "Tule please listen carefully son. Open Your Eyes, not to the world that you are looking at. Open Your Eyes to the world of pure being. Remember what you learned. Open Your Eyes inside, son, and meet me there!"

"Oh! Here we go, how do I do this? Let's see? Breathe, let go, remember, remember, remember....."

"Namaste again, Tule!"

"Oh! Namaste Lotus!"

"Now that you know where you are, maybe you want to go back with Wind?"

"Wait, wait! Not so fast you wise one. You still need to tell me who I am."

With a big belly laugh Lotus replied: "Tule what do you see I am?"

"You are a beaming rainbow, with a funny shape, sitting in contemplation on a flower, singing songs."

"Well, that is then what you are too: a beaming rainbow tree, with a funny shape sitting in contemplation on flowers, singing songs!"

"Say that again?"

"Tule you are me and I am you. All is a mirror image of the story I told you of creation. The miracle is that you can be standing tall on the surface of an Earth feeling Prana caress your branches, drinking from the waters of Yemaya, eating from your mother the Earth, crying every time you witness Ometecutli and

Omecihuatl dance at dawn and dusk. And all while you are alive! You just have to close your eyes and you will know only one truth, that you are the Rainbow Light that makes Universes exist. Inside you will find me seated at the East of your trunk observing it all, admiring it all. Through your trunk the two-feathered-dragons will dance as you breathe. Your roots will keep you solid and firm in the ground in red and orange; your trunk will shine yellow light helping you stand tall. Your middle will shine beautiful green and will mark the lotus seat. Your Top will be bright blue, indigo and purples as your branches extend tall to reach the sky, giving you sound to sing and an extra eye to see the unseen."

"Wow! I hope I remember all that."

"Tule, all you need to do is BE."

"That I can remember, all I need to do is BE. Just one more thing, why are my branches never naked like the other trees?"

"Because Tule you are the Tree of Life, you are the guide to all the other trees. Your existence reminds the other trees how leaves look and it gives them hope as they wait for them to grow again. There is one thing you need to know about Earth. Soon the time will come when not only trees will inhabit the Earth, but animals and birds. The animals will be your allies and they will nest in you and protect you. But as the code that you know now becomes more complex, other beings will inhabit the Earth. Two-legged beings. They will be tempted by the 6 demons of the underworld - desire, greed, jealousy, anger, depression and fear. Remember when fear took hold of you in the waters of Yemaya and you became deaf to my voice?"

"Yes I called you but I could not hear you, I was terrified, I was going to die."

"Exactly - you became afraid of death. Well, when we allow these demons to take over we become ignorant, blind and deaf. These beings will be challenged by ignorance and they will forget. In fear of death they will be capable of embodying the essence of any of the demons of the underworld. They will not see you as magnificent Tule, once their teacher and guide. They will see you as wood to cut to satisfy their desires. They will no longer see the sacred mountains of Kailas but piles of rock with precious metals and jewels to take away. They will no longer

see Yemaya. They won't be able to distinguish dawn from dusk, or cry at the sacred dance of light and darkness because they will permanently live under artificial light and screens. They will forget about Prana and pollute the air with toxic gases. They will treat the soil they walk on with disregard, killing anything in it. They will pray to distorted illusions of the Light and Ometeotl, deny the existence of Omecihuatl, mutilating the code of life, mutilating the second head of the feathered-dragon: darkness, feminine, silence, rest, stillness, emotion."

"Stop! How can this be possible? How can you allow this to happen?"

"There is a point in evolution where creation becomes co-creator and co-creators have a choice. They can choose to forget they are Light, that they are rainbow and colour and they can become grey, fearful, greedy, angry, and dance with the lord of the underworld instead of the Light."

"Why?"

"Because in ignorance we know no different, we are deaf and blind."

"Will they cut me into pieces?"

"Probably, yes. But remember you are more than wood, and even if they cut your wood they can never cut your Rainbowness away. Unless, of course, Tule you forget and become easy prey for the demons for the underworld."

"How can I not forget?"

"Be silent every day with me, ground your being in your empty heart, take the lotus seat and contemplate."

"Can I take that seat now?"

"That seat is always there for you to take. The only thing that can prevent you from sitting still on it is attachment and fear. If you remain attached to the wood that makes you Tule you will never be free to take the lotus seat. But if you fear death you will burn in an instant if you take the seat. Because fearing death is fearing life. When you fear death you are blind to the truth that there is nothing to fear because the universe is empty and the wood that makes you Tule is only like foam in a wave!

"Yes, of course, the code of life, zero emptiness, the beginning of it all, and the rest of it all. The beginning and the end of the outbreath; the beginning and the end of the inbreath."

"Wind is calling... it is time for you to open your eyes to the outside. Be Tule and teach the two-legged tribe to remember not to be afraid of death."

Tule started feeling the pull of the wind and felt dizzy. Before Tule knew it, he was inside the tornado that Wind was breathing, only this time descending. "Breathe Tule, Breathe with me."

Tule touched the ground and opened his big brown eyes to the outside, and saw not water but Yemaya in the distance; not the sky but Ometecutli and Omecihuatl waving at him; no more other trees but only himself, Tule, in different shapes and forms, with only Ometeotl holding them all together in their dance.

When dusk came Tule cried, as he knew himself to be one with the sacred feathered-dragons, performing the dance of Light and Darkness in a magnificent display of rainbow colours.

When night and rest came Tule closed his eyes to the outside and silenced with Lotus inside...only to hear one last teaching...

"...there is no Lotus, so don't take it all too seriously!"

Search for your forgotten VOICE or COLOURness, feel it, be it, dance it and then let it go and become RAINBOW, feel it, be it dance it and then let it go and become LIGHT, be still in it and then let it go and become EMPTY, then...dance with colour again.

Since the beginning of time many COLOURS have danced the sacred dances of the Earth - Yemaya, Tule, the Sun, the Rain, Fire, the Wind... Today, as we remember which dance we have danced before and with which COLOUR, we must not forget that the core message encrypted in **all traditions** follows a simple count of sacred order.

The Prana that gives life is the Prana that gives life; RED, YELLOW, ORANGE, GREEN, INDIGO, PURPLE or BLUE Prana, it does not matter, it is Prana.

In the same way indigenous wisdom and mysticism speak about core principles, and what is important is not the form and wrapping they come in but what is inside the wrapping. The feathers do not make the mystic (shaman, druid, healer, curandero) wiser, what makes the mystic wiser is to know it needs no feathers.

Some forgotten voices of indigenous wisdom and mysticism:

"Only those who are not deafened by fear can hear"
(your ancestors)

Ignorance is the source of suffering. Ignorance is when you forget that:

- The Universe is Empty
- All is One Breath. Impermanent, forever breathing, transforming and evolving.
- All follows rhythm. The rhythm of the breath, inbreath – outbreath.
- All is vibrating as One. Pure being. Interconnected.
- All is vibrating as Dual. Phenomena. The illusion of separation.
- Oneness and Duality always dance holding hands.
- All comes in a dual pair of opposites, which complement each other.
- All evolves from its previous; all is and has a cause and all is and has an effect. Karma.
- All there is, is 'me', all is a reflection of 'me'. Self-awareness. Detach. Nothing is personal.

- Death is an illusion; it means only transformation and transmutation. The world Bridger.
- All is a repetition of the 'One' code of life; macrocosm and microcosm are mirror-like reflections.
- All will meet at different times desire, jealousy, anger, depression, greed and fear. The awakened mind has choice in how it dances with these; the ignorant mind is a puppet of these demons.

Understanding in depth the written word, practicing and experiencing, the above will lead you to a life of non-violence, *Ahimsa,* and therefore liberation from suffering.

Tule
(Santa María
del Tule,
Oaxaca,
México)

*"You dream because you are asleep,
when you wake up,
you will stop dreaming
and then you will start living.*

*But if you forgot how to dream,
it will be very difficult for you
to waken up.
Because you do not know
you are asleep."*
Ná Áak

Chapter VI
Spiritual Sovereignty

When we look at the different meanings that a word has, we open the doors into where they come from, how they were born, where they were first used and what they described. As time goes by, we forget that every word we speak was created at some point in time for a specific purpose.

We speak as if we know what we are saying, while our attention is scattered, wondering about the past and the future, being completely absent from our speech. Most of the time we speak in automatic pilot to fill time or silence, and most of the time if we were asked to repeat what we were saying we would struggle to remember.

To enter deeper into the realm of this section, Lost Sovereignty, we need to explore and meditate on the words we are using:

LOST SOVEREIGNTY

LOST:
Not knowing what to do in a new situation;
Not knowing where you are and how to get to a place;
Derives from 'lessen' meaning to be made less strong.
If someone or something is lost, no one knows where it is;
As an adjective meaning confused.

SOVEREIGNTY:
To be self-governing;
Independent;
Having the highest power;
The ruler King or Queen of a nation;
Derives from Latin 'super' meaning above.

When I say 'LOST SOVEREIGNTY' I imply that our
'SOVEREIGNTY', our capacity to be independent, to self-govern, to have the highest power, to be 'above' or raise above, has

been 'L O S T', nobody seems to know where it is, we are confused, not knowing where we are, made less strong, diluted.

At some point in the journey of creation and evolution our ignorance made us choose to forget; our ignorance made us perceive and believe that we were separate and not one. In that moment, our capacity to be independent and to govern ourselves and our life evaporated and dissolved in the confusion of being lost.

The world we are experiencing today is, for the most part, a place where we have forgotten that we are all ONE. When we inhabit a human body we might perceive that separation is the only apparent and true reality. Many people choose to live trapped in illusions that become the only truth for them, just like in ROCK, COTTON or IRON realities. They work so hard to make sure that their reality does not get disturbed that anyone challenging that delusion is confronted and attacked, and the information dismissed.

There are many institutions that govern and rule in the world today from ROCK, COTTON or IRON realities. This has had a massive impact on the quality of life on Earth and just like it was said in the story of creation of Tule:

> *"The one who has Crystal clear awareness understands that the trinity is only a trinity because of the sacred union of one and two, Ometeotl and its consorts; the one essence of life and its dual manifestation as 'the mother' and 'the father' of all of creation. This is the eternal paradox that will permeate all forms that follow. This is the 'key-note' for harmonious creation.*
>
> *Dissonant and disharmonious creation will emerge if any of this, in ignorance, becomes denied and forgotten. As Ometecutli and Omecihuatl cannot exist separate from Ometeotl, so the trinity (3) cannot exist separate from its essential nature; union (1) and separation (2); pure being and phenomena."*

As many of these institutions have forgotten and because they have the need for everyone to stand under their belief, ignorance has proliferated like a pandemic on planet Earth making the masses live in fear and act out of fear. The institutions, knowing we suffer from attachment and greed, feed us just like someone would feed a beast

– from a distance, through screens and papers – plenty of raw meat, violence and drama.

As we saw in the story of the creation of Tule, separation is imminent in the universal dance. Catrina (Death) weaves the inbreath, the outbreath and the emptiness, allowing everything to manifest from the first breath of life. In order for this breath to happen, Ometeotl has to separate from the inside of White Lotus aided by Catrina, only then to die to its oneness and become Ometecutli and Omecihuatl. Everything needs to die to its "I AMness" to be able to become something else and therefore for the universe to exist. If at any point, any of the deities or forms decided not to cooperate and not to die to itself, all the creation and unfolding of the universe would stop and become stagnant and dissonant, slowly dying from suffocation. This is because what they have stopped, without realising it, is the primal pulse of life that allows all to exist: They have stop **breathing**, they have started **dying**!

Without separation, without death, there would never have been a first breath, a first quantum soup, a first 'mother' and 'father', a first earth, a first human being. It is only when the light shines through the prism that it becomes the diversity of colours that are displayed in a rainbow. The rainbow only exists because there has been *Separation-Death*.

Separation-Death triggers the experience of fear and anxiety. In order to separate we must die to the union we were part of. So as the universe explodes into being in a tremendous display of apparent destruction and separation, being dismembered into thousand-fold earths and thousand-fold suns; so we are dismembered and explode into being, at birth. Just like DaNA when she was chased by the monster in the waters and felt terrified of dying, so do we feel and experience the terror of death and separation as we leave the safe warm waters of the mother and come into the experience of being a sovereign breathing being.

Because we have experienced life in the water, because once we were one with the universal mother and the universal father, our Iceberg has crystals of water that contain the information of that experience. That information might be located, in our iceberg, above the water or below the water (conscious or unconscious), but no matter where we can find it the message is still visible on the surface. The message that we receive is the craving and longing for that deep experience of union and connection. We silently grieve our apparent separation.

When Ignorance takes hold of us and we completely forget about our previous experiences of union – that is, if we have made unconscious the experiences, burying them deep in the iceberg that lies underneath the water – the ever present longing, seeks to attain the experience of mystical union. We seek for anything around us that can bring similar experiences of connection; any experience that will kill the natural imperatives of the life of separation; anything that will numb the symptoms that we are separate so we can pretend that we are not.

The four natural imperatives of a separate life are:

- Pain
- Ageing
- Illness
- Death

These attributes of life are intrinsic to all sentient beings, and humans are sentient beings. We have senses that allow us to perceive reality and to process reality through sound, visuals, smells, taste and touch. It is this capacity to feel that helps us to experience pain as well as pleasure, illness as well as health, growth and ageing as well as birth.

We use these same senses to numb the painful symptoms using substances or behaviours designed to avoid the dreaded pain, illness, ageing and death. But the impulse and longing for connection is extremely strong and lasts throughout our lives. Some practical examples of this longing in action could be: the person that decides to have children to find meaning in life, and as the child is born the longing is fulfilled with the miracle of pregnancy and birth. After a few weeks, however, when the child keeps them awake all night and they realise the full demands and responsibility of parenthood, the old longing surfaces again. Another example could be the person that prefers to avoid pain through substances such as nicotine, alcohol, heroin, opium, etc. While under the effect of the substance the separation gets numbed down or forgotten, only to be woken up with vengeance the next day with a hangover.

This is just like we saw in Kamu's story where the community of Whales, because of the collective pain they experienced after the tragic massacre, allowed Planktohol to become the cure to the pain. This eternal cycle of un-fulfilment is what gives life to greed.

In the search for external fulfilment, this craving for union, we have transformed the mystical and spiritual nature of the experience of life into a fixed and solid institution – religion.

Let's allow ourselves to reflect again on the meaning of the words we are using:

M Y S T I C I S M
Deriving from the Latin word 'mysticus' implying: of, belonging to, used in sacred mysteries.
As a noun implies the belief that there is hidden meaning in life or that each human being can unite with God.

S P I R I T U A L I T Y
Deriving from the Church Latin word 'spiritualis' implying: spiritual, of the spirit; of breathing.
The above derives from the Latin word 'spiritus' implying: breath, breathing, air.
The above derives from the Medieval Latin word 'spirare' implying: breathe; blow; live.

R E L I G I O N
Deriving from the Classical Latin word 'religio' implying: reverence, respect, awe, supernatural constraint, taboo, obligation.
The above derives from the Latin word 'religare' implying: tie out of the way; bind fast; moor.
The above derives from the Late Latin word 'ligare' implying: to bind; to tie; bind, tie, fasten.

As a noun implies the belief in and worship of a god or gods, or any such system of belief and worship.

If we can imagine an experience of the words according to the meaning they have we could say that:

> The experience of **Spirituality** is possibly something
> close to the conscious experience of **breathing**.

> The experience of **Mysticism** is possibly something
> close to the conscious experience of **belonging**.

> The experience of **Religion** is possibly something
> close to the conscious experience of **binding**.

This is the main difference that we see when we look at religion and mysticism. In religion, as it is an institution, there is a set of handbooks or sacred scriptures that are to be followed as dogma, in their literal translation and failing to do so will imply punishment. This punishment normally comes in the form of burning hells, condemnation, excommunication or persecution and still today, in many cases, death.

When we look at the main religions that are institutionalised on Planet Earth, we can trace their teachings and practices back to mystical teachings and ancient wisdom. The mystical aspect of religion has remained true to the spirit of the original teachings of the prophet for which the religion is founded. In all of these mystical practices, the practitioner normally enters into a direct experience with the divine consciousness, god or light. Through trance, breathing, prayer, fasting or dancing they abandon the realm of ordinary linear time and space to enter into the realm of cosmic union and interconnection.

Many of these practices have remained occult and secret for generations for diverse reasons, one of them being persecution. In most cases, they would be the natural adaptation or evolution of the indigenous practices of the ancestors of each land.

Contrary to the individual pursuit of a direct experience of the divine, in religion the common factor is the role of the intermediary between the human being and the 'god'. This priest-like figure is the one appointed by the church to intercede for the common 'sinners' to help them find 'god's' forgiveness. If they have been good in following the church's manual, perhaps they can earn a little taste of the 'god' that they will never be, but can only aspire to be close to, by going to the church where 'it' is hidden away under lock and key, or displayed under the guidance of the intermediary during select 'festivals'.

In this system the common man or woman is already condemned without even knowing it. Their condemnation is that they will never be 'god'. Therefore, they can only be common human beings with the task of being faithful to the manuals so that they can be welcomed into the community of the church, aspiring to have a little taste of 'god' or to see 'it' in display.

In religion we find many rituals and prayers that have been adapted and trimmed down from their ancient indigenous roots to suit the purpose of the church. For example, baptism is a common ritual in most human cultures and many religions have different versions. Traditionally it was used to welcome the spirit of the person to the Earth and into the community. In many cases the person, normally a child coming into teenage years, would have to pass through different initiation rituals to overcome the fear of death. When the child overcame death, this proved that they had mastered the illusion of human life, and the symbolic ritual of welcoming – the baptism – would be performed so they could officially take up their role in the community.

In fact, in human life, ritual is useful to help us remain in touch with true reality – connection and oneness – and not the separation we perceive. On the other hand, in religious practice, ritual has become empty of spirit. The institution, due to its fixed and closed nature, stops evolving. Instead, it becomes stagnant and chokes the spirit of the original mystic belonging and spiritual breath.

Another important aspect of some religious institutions is their disharmonious mythology and deities. As we explored in the previous chapter and as nature would display, we can observe that: as life there is death, as night there is day, as masculine there is feminine, as light there is darkness.

One aspect or attribute cannot exist without its polar opposite. They belong to each other, becoming possible only because the other twin exists. This means that if the night did not exist then the day would never be born; so if darkness did not exist the light would never have been able to shine.

In these institutions, a common idea is that darkness and night are evil, bad, wrong and they are amputated from the main body of the divine source. The end product is a deity that is only good and light and never visits or shows the dark side, because the dark side represents devil, the unknown.

Followers of the religion are then taught to stay away from evil and the devil by closely following the church manual and sacred scriptures. Anything that does not sit right with the top intermediaries is added to the lengthy list of all things evil and bad. Normally what does not sit right with the leaders is a person, ideas or organisations that challenge, criticise or disturb their religion's purpose and ideals.

These types of religious institutions live mostly from the IRON reality, based on and locked into the position of:

"I AM RIGHT AND YOU ARE WRONG"

As we explored before, this position implies disagreement. 'War' becomes justifiable because those wrong and evil have to be exterminated. I am sure that there is no need to list evidence that human beings have fought and killed throughout the centuries because of religious beliefs. We have had many holy crusades, holy wars and holy inquisitions in different countries at different times from many different religious institutions, normally living from an IRON reality. It is said that almost a billion people have been killed because of these wars: 1,000, 000, 000 people, just like you and me, died in the hands of people that were GREY and decided to wash away, with torture and death, the COLOURness of individuals and cultures.

These actions made the different religions powerful, inducing pain and fear wherever they went. How can there be a deity that is all 'loving' behind those actions? I find it difficult to understand that we have chosen to forget what is inconvenient to remember. How can an institution that is designed to give the experience of binding set you free? If an institution has an IRON mentality (a mentality of power, fear and greed) as its back bone, how is that body going to grow and develop something that was never cultivated in it in the first place, something like generosity, charity, faith or love?

If I want to control someone I cannot love that someone because the act of controlling and binding that someone to my will is making him my slave, taking away his sovereignty. If I love someone I set them free, I make them sovereign and independent, I help them to think for themselves and to find their own experience of life and the divine. Joseph Campbell reminds us of this in the introduction:

> *"...Where there is a way or path, it is someone else's path.*
> *You are not on your own path.*
> *If you follow someone else's way, you are not going to*
> *realize your potential..."*

In one occasion I witnessed a conversation between a religious believer and a free thinker. The religious believer challenged the free thinker about not following the word of his god, and his religion. He explained in detail about the truth of the message of their prophet and how that prophet had come to save us 2000 years ago. He mentioned how if he did not follow and convert to his religion he would go to hell with the devil. The free thinker paused for a moment and then proceeded to ask: "As I do not understand fully your religion it would be ignorant of me to dismiss what you are saying. What I would like to understand is what your religion says about all the humans that lived on Earth before the prophet that saves you was born?" The reply the free thinker got was: "You see, that is why you are going to go to hell, because you ask questions that you should not ask. You must never question dogma. I will pray for your soul." The free thinker said: "Do you mind, while you are praying for me, to ask your 'god' how come there are fossils that date many thousands of years before your prophet came into the world?" The religious man, quite upset at this stage, said: "It was the devil that put them there to test our faith, and I can see that you have none, I pity you."

In these institutions the sacred scriptures are never actualised. The belief is that they have been channelled by 'god' and that they are the voice of 'god.' In many cases the message is taken literally, forgetting about the ever present use of metaphors, analogies and myth in the scriptures. When we look at the history of the scripture we commonly find that it was at a particular time in history when the man that decided to create the church chose randomly from different books and manuscripts to form the sacred book. What was not considered appropriate at the time was simply not included or maybe adapted to imply a different meaning. The myths and texts of all these sacred books are simply a compilation of ancient myths and teachings from the people indigenous to the land before they were conquered or converted.

That is why, if we read the Popol Vuh and the Book of Genesis in a christian bible, we can easily pin point the common elements, as we could if we compare them with sacred scriptures from different cultures. Religion took the myth out of the text and with it the magic and meaning of the text, making it solid, literal, fixed, definite and unchallengeable.

The other common factor to institutionalized religion is the aversion to sexuality and the feminine. In their cosmologies you can normally find a god father a god son or main prophet and some add 'grace' or a 'holy spirit' to complete a trinity. However, quantum physics, indigenous wisdom and mysticism all suggest that the trinity of the universe is characterised by one, unified field of consciousness, containing both mother and father within itself. The feminine gives birth to creation while the masculine is the impulse of creation. The father breathes and the mother gives birth and becomes the earth.

However, in these religious cosmologies it is hard to find the mother or the feminine in a prime role or position. She is normally apart and portrayed as a virgin because sex and the natural procreation functions were believed to be dirty and acts of the devil.

We know that without a mother no human being could possibly be born just as without the feminine no universe or Earth could possibly be born. In spite of the obvious, these religions amputated the myths to suit their purpose. It is almost amusing to find that in most of these religions it is only men who are allowed to be priest-like figures and intermediaries between the 'god' and the common people. Women are allowed to devote their lives to the church and 'god' but only serve as an adjacent branch of the main male-dominated religious hierarchy.

So far we have mutilated the arm of darkness and the arm of the feminine from the religious core. Just imagine what years of such teaching has done to humanity and to our iceberg? Imagine all the information that throughout the centuries has been added on to the unconscious iceberg underneath the water.

Moving on to the aspect of sexuality we find that some of these institutions require celibacy as part of the vows that the intermediaries commit to or that the ladies that choose to serve the church accept. The absence of a sexual life not for mystical purposes of asceticism, reflection or contemplation, but because it is 'dirty.' So men of god do not have a sexual life because they are men of god and women that serve the church do not have a sexual life because they are serving god. Failure to comply will mean mortal sin, where the forgiveness of god through a high-ranking intermediary is required to fix the problem. In this way all who are born are already considered to be out of grace because they come from a sexual act and because, as we heard before, they can never be 'god.' In that form they are sinful, they are born with original sin.

So if we add the third mutilation, now we have an institution that persecutes and kills what they consider evil, that denies the divinity and equality of the feminine and that denies sexuality.

In addition, in most cases the religion was made an institution, not at the request of the prophet that they preach to follow, but years after their death, as a political move to unite and control territory. The purpose of the institution, then, becomes infected with greed, except this is a different kind of greed, this is holy greed as it serves as a holy excuse to conquer new sinful land and make it holy; expand holy empires and convert barbaric people to the holy system. That is how the 'snakes' were expelled from many countries, just as saint Patrick (whom in fact was never officially made saint by his own religious institution) cleared all of the snakes from Ireland. That is how the land, once sacred to the indigenous population, was crowned by the new symbol of the institution in charge, freeing the place of COLOURNESS.

A world free of 'snakes', a world free of evil, free of feminine, free of sexuality, a GREY world for everyone free of COLOUR. It is interesting that the life-force energy or creative power of the universe in many mystical traditions is associated with dragon-snake figures and myths. An example is the yogic understanding of kundalini energy (snake paired couple) that raises from the base of the human body (the sexual centre) upwards trough the spine and provides life and creative power. Another analogy is the shape of DNA, the paired snake chain of amino acids, the biological source of life, resembles a snake. Coincidentally, this form is what is mostly associated with evil in institutionalized religions. The force of temptation and perdition is always portrayed as a snake and/or a woman. The perfect combination to cease life, eliminate DNA and the Womb that gives birth to it; life truncated and made stagnate.

Sometimes I wonder if this information was known by some at the Top and perhaps, knowing the amazing potential that life force had, they decided to eradicate it from their cosmology. I don't consider it particularly important to confirm this because it's clear that a population afraid of evil and burning in hell, afraid of sexuality, afraid of the feminine (emotion and nurturing) and afraid of asking questions, is easy to control, convert and conquer. People who do now know they are divine and believe that they are dirty simply for being born, are easy to control if you are the only one with the key to open the box where 'god' is kept. I do have to give credit to such an impeccable system, which works so effectively to gain power and wealth by inducing fear, by stealing peoples' sovereignty and capacity to think by themselves.

This chapter would not be complete without mentioning the effects that an institution of this nature has. A system that truncates and suffocates life cannot live harmoniously or in balance. A system that stops the universal flow becomes a cancer to the body, because as the flow is truncated there is no more life breathed into it. As this happens the internal cells in need of breath become hungry ghosts in need of fresh air. In common language this can be heard in the voices that have been the target of the hungry ghosts: sexual abuse (a majority of boys under 11 years of age); ritualistic abuse (like rape to children under 13 years of age); psychological and physical abuse (from orphanages to secondary schools); and so on. Clear statistics cannot be found and different reports are released from the institutions and the organisations helping the survivors. In my understanding, in countries where the institutions controlled education unilaterally, the statistic in some countries shows that 1 in 4 children have been forced to have a sexual interaction with members from these religious institutions.

Some of these institutions have taken time to acknowledge the inappropriate behaviour of their members, implementing solutions to prevent these painful and horrific acts from ever happening again. This is an example of one of these institutions' top leader's response:

> "...At the conclusion of my meeting with the ... bishops, I asked that Lent this year be set aside as a time to pray for an outpouring of God's mercy and the Holy Spirit's gifts of holiness and strength upon the Church in your country. I now invite all of you to devote your Friday penances, for a period of one year, between now and Easter 2011, to this intention. I ask you to offer up your fasting, your prayer, your reading of Scripture and your works of mercy in order to obtain the grace of healing and renewal for the Church in .... I encourage you to discover anew the sacrament of

Reconciliation and to avail yourselves more frequently of the transforming power of its grace." From the Vatican, 19 March 2010, on the Solemnity of Saint Joseph BENEDICTUS PP. XVI

Most of the individuals who committed the abuse have been transferred to another area or country or quietly asked to leave the institution. The survivors have been given free counselling, a financial compensation with a confidentiality clause attached, warned not to speak.

The reality is that every day as people attend their church they get their sins forgiven, their piece of god and blessing from an intermediary that lives in the incongruence of a vow of celibacy to which they cannot commit, and a religious institution that speaks about unconditional love and yet gives a hand book of conditions to be loved.

Our challenge today is to break free from the binding chains of fear and embrace our own personal, unique and individual

SPIRITUAL SOVEREINGTY

We need to be aware that if we wish a new spirituality to emerge, first we need to stop the storm of the religious binding that each of our icebergs has accumulated since the beginning of religion. Then, once the storm of truncated cosmologies has been conciliated, we can re-emerge with a new mystical and spiritual life. If we do not wish to consider this, then everything we create will still carry poison of holy greed and holy fear of the feminine, of the darkness and of the creative source of all life, our sacred sexuality.

We can already see the effects of this in the new self-help and holistic approaches emerging, where they pathologically deny negativity, darkness and evil, just like religion.

The practitioner is taught to place positive thinking and divine angels on top of anger, depression, grief, etc. The result: no-different than taking a headache pill or drinking a pint of alcohol, immediate numbness and denial that the anger, depression, grief are still there and at some point will ask to be addressed and conciliated. Remember:

> *"No problem can be solved from the same level of*
> *consciousness that it was created"*
> *(A. Einstein)*

Ask the questions you need, search for the information that you require and become a believer, a believer in yourself, a believer in your own path, find your Breath, your Spirit and become a Mystic by Belonging to your Sovereign Self.

"In the beginning
That was non-existence,
Only potential energy at rest,
Unmanifest,
Formless, nameless,
From 'That'
Emerged
'What is'.
'That' made itself its Self,
It was Self-Created
Was a flavour,
A taste and look for beauty.
After perceiving beauty
One can experience pleasure.
Who would breathe, exhales.
In that Love Dwells Brahman.
It did not exist in only the
Ether of the Heart centre
Within another centre.
He alone causes Grace.
When the devotee finds
Freedom from fear,
Rest and trust in 'That' Power
Which knows the way
To Self-Realization,
Invisible,
Bodiless,
Undefined,
Unsupported,
Then he has touched Brahman
The Courageous"
(The Taittiriya Upanishad)

Chapter VII
Socio-Political-Economic
Sovereignty

After exploring the Spiritual aspect of life and how, from the original experience of union and belonging, we created religious institutions that meant binding; it is fair to presume that the institutions that have been created to rule human beings in a social context, in a political context and in an economic context might follow a similar history. For that purpose let's look at the etymology and different meanings that are attached to the words 'Society', 'Politics' and Economy:

S O C I E T Y
From the Latin 'societas' meaning: joint pursuit, alliance, partnership.
From the Latin 'socius' meaning: associate, companion, ally, sharing.

The friendly association with others.
Congregation, assembly, union.

P O L I T I C S
From the Latin 'politicus' implying: of the state.
From the Greek 'polites' implying: a townsman.
From the Greek 'polis' implying: a town.

The science of good sense, applied to public affairs.
Also meaning politeness, civility.
To be present and ready, to stand by, to support, be favourable to.
A kindness, a favour or a service.

E C O N O M I C S
From the Latin 'oeconomicus' implying: orderly and methodical.
From the Greek 'oikonomos' meaning: house-distributor or overseer.
From the Greek 'nomos' meaning: law, name, regulation.

Something that you do in order to spend less money.
Careful use of money, time or goods so that nothing is wasted.

The system by which a country's money and goods are produced and used.

Attentively and carefully managing goods or money.

From the meaning and etymology of these words one would understand that the experience of Society, Politics and Economy would include in one way or another, the following:

SOCIETY:
A friendly alliance or partnership, union.

POLITICS:
Attention to public or civil matters by the state.

ECONOMY:
Careful use of resources, so nothing is wasted.

When we explore the territory of Socio-Political-Economic Sovereignty in present times we encounter the same paradigm that was discussed before from religious institutions. We are simply looking into the window of different fields and aspects of life and living, but the human beings that have created the systems and the institutions are the same as the ones that created the religious institutions. The same human beings who silenced and then forgot about the voices that were controversial in spirituality have followed the same path in all other areas of life.

Our present Social, Political and Economic institutions have been created with a consciousness of fear. If we can recall the story of the RAINBOW people from chapter II where GREEN, infected by desire, jealousy, greed, depression, anger and fear, decided to get rid of RED, eventually creating a GREY world with no colour. In that story we can clearly see the split that occurred in the psyche of GREEN as it forgot it was a RAINBOW colour reflecting from the one Light. In that moment as GREEN understood itself to be separate from the rest of colours and separate from the Light it believed:

"I AM RIGHT and YOU ARE WRONG"

Once we create institutions based on a split, there will always be two sides in confrontation, war always latent and eventually imminent. Today the world is a world that has grown 'split' from itself (RAINBOW) and from its source (Light). The split has gotten so big that the times of denial and covering up the existence of a RAINBOW and the Light are far gone and forgotten. Today we live in a world where we know GREY as our only true, scientifically proven and statistically correct reality. The mere suggestion of the existence of of RAINBOW people or the Light, are in the category of:

> Social Psychotic Paranoid Schizophrenic
> Political Terrorism
> Economic Communism

We are so far removed from the source that the world has become fixed in a reality of 'splits', where war, confrontation, imprisonment, medication or persecution are **necessary** and **correct**. Today it is **normal** and **accepted** to kill, torture and silence any human being who behaves or thinks differently from 'GREY'; **because we do not see human beings behaving or thinking differently, but rather we see:**

> Psychotic Communist Terrorists
> ITS (things)
> ENEMY
> THE AXIS OF EVIL

Our previous consciousness state of.....

> 'I AM RIGHT and YOU ARE WRONG'

......has changed, without us even noticing, to a consciousness of severe gravity that screams:

> 'WE ARE RIGHT and 'IT' IS THE ENEMY'

There is no longer individual thinking as 'I AM', identifying with my 'I AMness', but what we have is a 'GREY' machine that has indoctrinated the 'I's' into a non-identity GREYNESS, into 'WE are GREY'.

This GREY thinking and behaviour eradicates 'YOU' from existing, because all they tolerate is what lies within the boundaries of GREY. What remains outside this boundary is the enemy of the GREY machine.

We have allowed a world to exist, which is composed of the 'INside circle' of GREYS and the world of the 'OUTside circle'. This OUTside circle is not even a world or people; it is a world of $\overline{IS}$, unknown and unwanted by all. That is how ignorance and not knowing transforms 'YOU' into $\overline{I}$.

Once the GREY machine successfully $\overline{I}$-alises, 'YOU', then all who lives INside the circle automatically become blind, because INside the circle is also empty of 'YOU' and full of $\overline{IS}$, so any other reality apart from the one GREY $\overline{I}$-alised world is the ENEMY. In that way 'WE' INside the circle no longer see human beings OUTside the circle. Now 'WE' only see 'inanimate objects' OUTside GREY, which are treated as such.

These inanimate objects, these $\overline{IS}$ that live OUTside the circle, are the ENEMY because anything outside GREY represents a threat to the existence of GREY. Think about it, it is common sense. If anything exists and lives and survives outside GREY then how can you justify GREY being the only omnipotent government, economy or society? As we explored before, how can you justify, then, only one true religion, if there are many religions outside the one true religion? That is why the simple existence of OUTside the circle is a challenge for the survival of the great GREY machine. Therefore the OUTside has to become the EVIL ENEMY.

To the eyes of those INside the circle, what lies OUTside is not human or alive, but simply objects to be removed and destroyed. So today $\overline{IS}$ - once of Light, once of Rainbow, once 'YOU', human, alive, are now reduced to

COLLATERAL DAMAGE [*Hashim Kamel Radi 22, Jalal al-Yussuf 17, Alternet 08, Ibrahim al-Yussuf 12, Alternet 08, Ahmed Al-Rahal, Sufian al-Batayneh, Abdullah al-Ababneh, Ahmad al_enezi, Omran al-Serihaine, Fateha Ghazzi 8, Nada Abdallah 16, Um Aqeel-Khalil, Sahar Khalil, Khowla Abdel-Fattah 70, Samad Rabai, Faris El Baur 11, Saif El Baur, Marwa Abbas, Tabarek Abbas 8, Safia Abbas 5, Qassem Moussa, Thamer Abdel-Wahid 27, Nujah Abdel-Ridda 27, Najia Hussein, Haytham, Arkan Daif 14, Walid Abu Shaker,*

Hilal Faraj Silo, Manal SaadAllah, Mahroosa, Valentina Bashar, Samar Hussein 13, Mohammad Ahmed 4, Nadia Kalaf 33, Zeena Akram Hamoodi 12, Mustafa Akram Hamoodi 13, Zain El Abideen Akram Hammodi 18, Zainab Akram Hamoody Hamoodi 19Hassan Iyad Hamoodi 10, Ammar Muhammad Hamoodi 1Noor Elhuda Saad Hamoodi, Wissam Abed Hamoodi 40, Ihab Abed 34, Khairiah Mahmoud Basra 5, Kamaran Abdurazaq Muhamed, Duaa Raheem 6, Sa'la al-Mousai 55, Alaa-eddin Khazal 42, Wadhar Handi 34, Bashir Handi 28, Safa Karim

11, Sena Hassad 36, Rana Hassad, Maria Hassad 7, Sama Sami 30, Lana Sami Under 10, Miriam Sami Under, Lava Sami Under 10, Salma Amin 50, Mohammed Amin 27, Said Amin 24, Shams Amin, Sami, Tareq, Taras Protsyuk, Jose Couso 37, Vatche Arslanian 48, Hanna Fatah 70, James, Nicolas Kachadoorian, Edmund Kachadoorian, Wael Sabah, Noor Sabah 12, Abdul Khader 5, Hamsa Mohammed Omar 6, Hamsa Mohammed Omar 12, Ali Ramzi 10, Abu Salam Abdul Gafir 16, Rowand Mohammed Suleiman 8-months, Haithem Tamini 7, Nora Tamini 9, Arkan David Belu 28, Khansaa Thaib, Muhammed al-Barheini 25, Rashid Majid, Ghassan Majid, Arkan Majid, Uday al Shimarey, Dana Ali 8, Lamiya Ali 6, Abdullah Abdul-Majeed al-Sa'doon 26, Salman Abu al-Heel 25, Waleed Saleh Abdel-Latif 32, Tuamer Abdel Hamid 47, Hussein Rashid 18, Sa'aleh al-Jumaili son, Ghanem al-Jumali son, Mohtam 14, Rneed Amar 13[f]4, Daoud Daib, Ahmed al Kifan 17, Din Bulbili 15, Dwaine McGriff 69, David J. 39, Marc P. Derobien 19, Scott E. Barrett 24, Rudy H. Christofossis, Carlos F. Edi 25, David J. Smith 25, Zachary D. Smith 23, Lance Cpl. Timothy J. Poole 21, Daniel M. Angus 28, Jeremy M. Kane 22, Xin Qi 15, Thaddeus S. Montgomery 29, Gifford E. Port Jr 29, Adam K. Ginett 23, Josef Busk 65, Juan [sic] Nisenbaum 21, Dr. Siegfried SchwelaChaim Richter 81, Samuel Mandel 74, Dr. Entress Ernestine Hochfelder 70, Josef Hoffmann 89, Abraham Stieber 79, David Reichman 70, Tibor Pollak Albert Janos 48, Gerszon Wajsbort Armin Horn 70, Tadeusz Jaworski 19, Abraham Trijtel 14, Jettchen Fuld 67, Salomon Serlui 67, Renö Hirschfeld 64, Freide [sic] Littmann 70, Wolf Eisenhöndler 14, Josephine Kohn 69, Emil Kaufmann 78, Julius Sonnenberg 65, Abraham Blok Franz Waitz 67, Josef Daniel18, Max Lichtenstaedt Peter Diessenberg babyJohanna Seiner 72, Zeli Gieclik 34, Perla, Thomas, Stan, Pablo, XiChen, Lala, Omar, Carmen, Nick, David, Moises, Elena, Itzchel, Sage, Amir, Jordan, Patrick, Miguel, World War I 15,000,000, Russian Civil War 9,000,000, Stalin's Regime 20,000,000, World War II 63,000,000:Soldiers: 22, 000,000,Civilians in camps 12,000,000+, From hostilites, blockade, epidemics, hunger 16,000,000+, From bombing 1,500,000+, Hitler regime 6,000,000, Post war expulsion of Germans 2,100,000, Chinese Civil War 2,500,000, Mao Zedong's regime 40,000,000, Ocupation of Tibet 600,000, Congo free estate 8,000,00, Mexican Revolution 1,000,000, Armenian Masacres 1,500,000, First Chinesse Civil War 5,000,000, Korean War 3,000,000, North Korea Regime 3,000,000, Rwanda and Burundi 1,350,000, Second Indochina War 4,200,000, Ethiopia 2,000,000, Nigeria 1,000,000, Bangladesh 1,250,000, Cambodia 1,650,000, Mosambique 800,000, Afghanistan 1,800,000, Iran-Iraq War 700,000, Sudan 1,900,000, Kinshasa Congo 3,800,000, Spanish Civil War and Franco Regime 465,000, India 500,000, Algeria 537,000, Sudan 500,000, Vietnam 365,000, Angola 500,000, Ugandan Bush War 350,000, Sadam Hussein 300,000, Kurdistan 300,000, Liberia 250,000, Iraq international embargo 350,000, Bosnia and Herzegovina 175,000, Somalia 400,000, Hiroshima and Nagasaki 137,000]

This is NOT Collateral Damage! These are human beings just like you and me, who died because someone decided that they wanted more goods, more land, more power, more, more, more. All slaughtered like live stock on the sharp metal claws of GREED.

Death is a part of life and the way we die mirrors the way we live. When I look at this list, my chest explodes in rage and grief! It does not show people dying in the arms of their families in peace, but human beings being denied the right have a life. It shows that we live immersed in FEAR, GREED and IGNORANCE. Those who died were not ITS! They were **ME**! I died with each one of them and I continue to die every day as their voices get forgotten and we sit in the comfort of the chair of numbness.

We have been well indoctrinated by the powerful media and marketing of the GREY machine, and we have memorised the face of the 'enemy' and any threats to our plastic, glittery and effortless world. We are afraid, afraid to burn in hell for eternity because the place GREY describes is horrific, and we are terrified of the devil. We want to be rid of the 'Axis of evil' as it threatens our GREY countries and institutions. We blindly support the extermination, by any possible means, of the ENEMY. We become IT-alised human beings, living in PAPER reality (Chapter III) where we adapt to what we are told, following someone else's path to our death.

The paradigm that we encounter today is harder than it would have been centuries ago. Today, we have no recollection of where human beings come from, or where words, laws, constitutions, dogma, or religion originated from. Instead we suffer from the cancer of **no-thinking**. This identity-less being, anesthetised and numb, has no intention or desire to ask questions or become informed.

The world has entered into such a lethargic state that human beings have forgotten they can think for themselves. We have become the by-product of fear and greed, simply serving as little plastic soldiers, full of silicone implants, a chess game played by the few at the very, very top. These few leaders control dogma, beliefs, law, food, water, energy, fuel, communications, what we wear, what we watch on television and what we hear on the radio. And we comfortably sit on the sofa to be spoon fed by the disharmonious but convincing rhythm of the GREY machine.

We are Numb to Life!

Today it has become **anti**-social-political-religion-economical to have a different opinion, and even to **ask questions about the way we have been told we should live**. Families **silence** their children if they dare to think for themselves and split from the herd by questioning the big GREY systems that have fed them for years.

Friends alienate each other if they do not dress or behave GREY and communities bully and discriminate against non-GREY people.

This lifestyle works in your favour very well, that's if you are GREY and not the ENEMY. But the rule book of what is GREY and what is the ENEMY change constantly because the institution needs to survive and therefore any new threat has to be annihilated. What would happen if it becomes anti-GREY:

To be white	To use cash currency
To be gay	To produce your own
To be pregnant	electricity
To be rich	To grow your own vegetables
To be thin	To be unable to pay a
To be blonde	mortgage
To wear diamonds	To speak English ?...

The rules can change anytime because they adapt according to the needs of the institution that is in power.

> *"Those who want victory against terror without addressing underlying grievances, want an unending war"*
> *(Ami Ayalon; N.Chomsky-Hegemony or Survival)*

If we wish to have an education system that educates and not indoctrinates; a society that implies partnership and not discrimination; politics that take care of public affairs and not play games of deceit with the public; and an economy that promotes the best possible use of resources with no waste instead being profit-driven; then we have to address the underlying grievances and expose the inside of the machine that is in operation now. We need to allow the surrogate machine to collapse and die, then, as with our Spiritual Sovereignty, we will be able to reclaim our Social Sovereignty, our Political Sovereignty and our Economic Sovereignty. Trying to fix an old cloth will only be a waste of time and resources. We need to recognise that the cloth is torn and old, and only then can we let go of it, and knit a new one that suits the needs of the Planet and the population that lives in it.

I see more and more consciousness emerging that is allowing the old to die, because of the lethargy and numbness, and the incapacity to take collective responsibility for what humanity has been and what humanity has done up until now. But the young that are driving the change are looking for a quick and easy solution to 'buy' themselves out of the mess that has been created.

Our younger generations have no idea how to knit. They only know how to buy. Will they be wise enough to ask the elders and be taught? Or will they simply buy into another GREY machine system, only this time instead of a new version of the Roman empire, what we will possibly see is a new version of the empires from the stars.

Today we allow those in power to steal what belongs to the people; to declare war on an ENEMY country; to set the boundaries of a country, dividing the land as they please, believing it belongs to them. Our leaders have, either wisely or genuinely, forgotten that the Planet does not belong to anybody or anything. Planet Earth is Sovereign, as is the Universe. We believe the illusion that has been programmed into us, that the land (the Earth) and the people (human beings) belong to the State. When a mother gives birth to a child, who does the child belong to? The mother or the State? When you study birth certificates and their origin, you can very easily discover that in many GREY systems, your birth certificate means that you belong to the State; you belong to the GREY machine, and become a private company that can be bought and sold in the stock market. So are we human beings? Are we 'I' or 'YOU'? Or are we ITS? Are we inanimate property belonging to the GREY machine?

The land, once free, has been taken hostage, only to be sliced and sold to the highest bidder. Those in power secure control of the rich areas containing mines, resources and deposits of precious liquids (water and oil) or minerals. It doesn't matter which circle inhabited the land before the GREY machine arrived, if they want it they take it, no apologies made.

Banks and financial markets exist out of thin air, simply numbers on a screen, sums being transferred from account to account, always multiplying to the gain of those who control the game. Booms, recessions and depressions, all easily manufactured and controlled by introducing simple and complex algorithms into a computer. We have given these financial institutions the power to lend to us currency, but in reality they lend us empty numbers that move from one screen to the next. Producing in abundance, the essential nectar that feeds these institutions:

DEBT

We vote, believing that the system is democratic, only for our votes to be revoked and recounted every time they give the incorrect result. Referendums are called to repeat the voting procedure so it meets the institution's demands. But the game has been laid out so well, that many people become upset when they hear this, because they cannot afford to even consider that their vote does not really count and that things are always fixed at the top. The numbness and lethargy makes us respond like robots: "I put in my vote, X won, that's ok, it was democratic; head down, bottom up and keep ploughing." Again, no need or desire to ask the question: what does democracy mean? Is the decision really democratic when the majority was in opposition to X? Or why do I have to vote again?

The GREY institution seems merciful and caring just like a mother, so it provides us with wages that can be spent INside the circle of GREY, and only asks for a tiny piece of contribution back, TAX. In this manner the economy of the GREY machine can be simplified in a few lines and equations that even a young child can figure out:

For those who have time to entertain a few examples and mathematical common sense...

Choose from the following:

Essentials for your survival in the machine:
Tax = 2; Food = 3; House = 6; Transport = 2; Energy = 5; Total = **18**

Special features:

Health = 20	Holidays = 30	Pampering = 25
Leisure = 10	Sports = 25	Silicone = 60
Drugs = 25	Domestic appliances = 30	

Choose an income:
a) **10** minimum wage, full time
b) **30** professional degree, full time
c) **120** top player, full time

A Wages 10 - Essentials 18 = **Debt -8**
For A there is not much hope, but making sure it does not lose its job, and the aspiration to anything more than surviving becomes an impossible dream INside the system.

B Wages 30 - Essentials 18 - Extras 90 = **Debt -78**
For B it becomes more difficult to keep the lifestyle and is in a bigger deficit that A. B has a lifestyle that includes health and social living which complicates the balance at the end of every month.

C Wages 120 - Essentials 18 - Extras 225 = **Debt -123**
For C the numbers become big but it has an advantage, C is liked by the financial institutions because it has spending capacity.

What happens automatically INside the GREY circle is that the **ITS** need the numbers on the screen to be able to afford the services that the GREY machine provides because using services outside from the machine means going OUTside the circle and therefore becoming the ENEMY that needs to be punished. So with the freedom that is left, **ITS** approach the financial institutions and ask for a loan to cover their debts [*A needs 8 to barely survive; B needs 78 to maintain the lifestyle; C needs 123 but will ask for 500 to do further investments*], and after detailed scrutiny the financial institutions reply:

To A: *"I'll give you 8 but you will really owe me 11 with the interest. If you do not repay on time I will reposes what you have".*

To B: *"Yes of course, I'll give you 120 so you have some cash flow. In reality you will owe me 200 with the interest but do not worry because you will probably die before you finish repaying me; so we will add an extra 20 for life insurance so your debt is cleared in case you drop death of a heart attack".*

To C: *"Hello **IT**! Great to see you!, are you free for lunch? I know a great place for steak and good wine. I will give you the 500 you want, but why don't I add another 500 that I have to launder for Mr. **IT** and in that way we can buy the land beside your development too!"*

This is a simplified version of what we experience around financial institutions in the GREY machine, where everyone is respected in accordance to their monetary value. This is before we account for what happens when someone at the very top inputs the algorithm for recession in the computer.

In that case we see things like the 10 are no longer 10 but 8 because of inflation and services do not drop accordingly, rather they increase. From one day to the other instead of 16 to survive you need 20, but you still have your original salary of 8? Figure that out?

Another common algorithm normally used in recessions is tax increases from 2 to 4 and again salaries do not increase so the society of ITS spirals into enormous debt. This debt multiplies the numbers in the computers of those in control, interestingly enough always translating into profit.

Things turn nasty when the financial institutions then want their repayments and cannot get them because ITS cannot afford to pay back. That is when the financial institutions get in trouble too.

A mess like this normally becomes a long cat and mouse chase that ends up in the hands of a GREY legal system or, as it is happening today in many countries, death by suicide.

The GREY legal system has ITS dressed in black cloaks with funny wigs, making law and imparting the justice of GREY greed. If you're in any way trapped in the web of this system, you are probably guaranteed to lose, meaning more financial penalties, imprisonment or punishment, in some countries even by death; strangely if you are honest it does not necessarily plays on your favour, and if you are poor you have practically no chance of winning.

But if you have the ability to tell the men in cloaks what they want to hear or the capacity to buy a good lawyer that can do that for you, then most likely, it will not matter whether you are guilty or innocent, you will escape, with minimum or no loss.

Court houses are about written law and following this to the letter. When T̲S̲ are taken to court because they cannot pay back, the system is not interested that they cannot pay the debt; or that they no longer have energy to heat their home; or that their child is ill and they can't afford the 'luxury' of medical attention; or that they have no food on the table that day. Once in front of the man with the cloak and the wig all that matters is written law. If written law says their debt to the financial institution has to be paid. The man in the cloak looks for payment. If T̲S̲ cannot pay, their home is taken, their car, their furniture, anything that can repay what was owed. And if it does not amount enough, the debt will remain in their names and they will have no chance of borrowing money from any financial institution again.

Remember somebody on the minimum wage can barely survive in the GREY system, even if they work full time. People are getting paid according to written rules a wage that cannot cover the basic cost of living.

90% of the population of Planet Earth lives on roughly €5 a day. While the men in cloaks and wigs, the guardians of justice, simply read the law and enforce the law.
Justice? Of course it is just and fair, it follows written law!
May I ask, then, who wrote this law?

We might never finish this chapter if we try to address that particular question, but one thing I am sure of: the law was written by the same consciousness that made religion, politics, and economics - the consciousness of:

GREED	ANGER	DEPRESSION
DESIRE	JEALOUSY	FEAR

Although I have searched through history for a time when COLOURS or GREY T̲S̲ attained liberation and enlightenment and from that place wrote all the rule books of religion, law, constitutions, education and economics, I have not found it yet. All I can find so far is GREY rulebooks written out of GREED and FEAR. To my disappointment what I found was that our lady of Justice had gone to bed with GREED, with all of the other muses.

Although any six-year-old could figure out that the system is not equal or fair, we **ITS** sit in front of the big screens observing the leaders make the decisions that will affect our entire lives and we say:

> "It was democratic, I gave my vote."

If the regime of the western world would openly admit that is far from a capitalist and democratic institution, and more like a dictatorship, at least there would be some honesty.

> The danger of western thinking is the
> **illusion of freedom**.

When living in a communist or fascist regime or when under a dictatorship, every **IT** knows that they are not free, but oppressed. There are no false pretences; one makes the decisions and all have to follow. Maybe there is no choice in the variety of clothes to buy or cars or houses but at least **ITS** know that they have been made **ITS** and therefore they can choose to do something about it. At the doors of the different safari parks we can find guards checking the papers of the lions that want to come in or go out. The rule for permitting this exchange of lions into different safari parks is simply based on how many more servants and slaves the top 1% of the population needs.

> *A revolution can only start if people*
> *know they are being oppressed*.

When **ITS** can feel the rage of being oppressed then action can be chosen in a non-violent form. In recovery from trauma a natural stage is to be able to feel anger, because it is in that moment when the person realizes the depth of the trauma and wakes up from dissociation or paralysis into life again. Anger is not to be the fuel of action but its transmutation into compassion can give the person the strength to stand up and speak up.

But when **ITS** believe that their systems are free and democratic when in fact they are living under a dictatorship; very little can be done to stop the monopoly of power. In the west the dictators have built for us beautiful safari parks, full of attraction and glitter; parks where we can choose from infinite different things; but we are trapped. They control the supplies that come into the park, they control the lighting, the water, the distribution, the plots of land, and what is permitted or not permitted. In the safari park there are guards controlling order and law. Any upheaval showing signs of Psychotic Paranoid Schizoid behaviour, or Political Terrorism or Economic Communism, is confronted and put down by the anti-riot special forces.

All animals live happily ever after as long as no one ever asks questions like: why are we in a safari park and not in the wild? Why do we have to be confined to this area because we are yellow or black? Why do we have to eat what you produce and not our own home-grown food? Why can't we have what you have?, etc.

Who has more chance of breaking free: the lion that has lived in a cage and knows it is a prisoner or the lion that lives in a cage so large that it never even realises it is a prisoner?

The Story of the Gigantic Spider

As the COLOUR world was coming to an end the GREY machine had been slowly designed and gradually developed. This machine was built to conquer and alienate COLOUR. The new GREY emperors, thirsty and hungry for power set out on a quest to expand the domain of GREY and destroy any other COLOURS by swallowing them.

GREY drank from the holy grail of GREED, full of a dark, black, sticky vile substance that produces fire. This black oil helped the machine to move and grow, making it into a Gigantic Spider that marched across the globe killing trees, oceans, animals, valleys, mountains, and enemies as it spat fire and concrete, destroying everything in its way.

The Gigantic Spider gave the GREY leaders a taste of power and, intoxicated by it, they became like gods, encouraging reverence to the machine and using all that the Spider swallowed to produce goods, pleasure and food for the Spider itself and its leaders.

*In exchange, the **ITS** now eaten by the monster and working for the monster received currency to buy goods, pleasure and food (originally theirs but taken by the Spider) from the big GREY Machine.*

As a sign of reverence and respect to the Gigantic Spider, 'tax' had to be paid for receiving the currency and for spending the currency. This tax was the insurance that the leaders astutely created to keep the Spider alive.

As time passed, the machine became larger and more powerful with every turn of the calendar wheel.

*Once swallowed into the belly of the Spider, it didn't take long for the GREY people (once RAINBOW people) to see the benefits of having a Gigantic Spider as a surrogate mother. This machine organised everything; created the law and the rules; built the streets; produced the cars they drove; printed the currency and counted it; organised education and wrote history books for the children to study the ways of the GREY machine. It provided food in big supermarkets, so nothing had to be harvested and nothing needed to ripen naturally; everything was ready-to-use and ready-to-go. It used technology to facilitate labour and, with the press of a button, life became simple and effortless. The machine provided plenty of leisure and activities for **ITS** to keep them occupied: fashion, make-up, houses, cars, sports, sex, music, etc. This surrogate mother Spider eventually replaced Mother Earth, once honoured by the RAINBOW people. Now, instead of RAINBOW people and COLOURS living with the Earth in one beautiful, harmonious symphony, the Gigantic Spider sucked the life and resources of Mother Earth, in order to spit fire and concrete and manufacture* *artificial life for GREY* ͞IͨTͨSͧ; *only to defecate toxic waste filling the holes that its sharp claws left.*

In GREY world nobody had to think. They all were told what to do and when to do it. Children stopped walking on grass and only walked on the concrete spat out by the spider. It all became neat, controlled and sanitised. Life became simple and effortless. All you had to do obey and defer to the Machine by giving it your goods, pleasure and food and, of course, by paying tax as you bought all of them back.

As time went by, two major effects became imminent:
1) *Other circles started creating their own GREY machines shaped like big monsters, to protect and defend themselves against the Gigantic threat. Some of these new machines were made to confront and destroy the Spider.*
2) *The population of* ͞IͨTͨSͧ *inside the Spider exponentially grew with time and made it unstable, as there were too many to control and provide for.*

As resources became scarce inside the Spiders womb; the big machine needed to guarantee its survival by getting its hands on more resources now protected by other big Spiders. At the same time they needed to reduce the population inside it so it could continue to be sustainable.

Anyone who had resources became the ENEMY of the Gigantic machine because those resources gave the ENEMY the potential to create another Spider or the power to stop the Gigantic Spider.

The solution that the pilots of the Gigantic Spider figured out so it could continue spiting fire and concrete, was to create advanced weaponry. This weaponry was to guarantee the successful destruction of the ENEMY. This action only lead to the same counter-reaction from the ENEMY as it struggled to defend itself and avoid death in the jaws of the GREY Spider.

All monster machines from all the corners of the Planet became not only capable of spitting fire and concrete; but capable of firing missiles and small metal balls that could engulf the Earth in a mushroom cloud of heat and radiation.

The Planet filled with tension and fear as Spiders played games and tested their weapons, sending their plastic soldiers to fight against the plastic soldiers of other spiders.

It did not take long for some astute GREY Spider leader to see the profit in manufacturing weaponry and offering it to all Spiders. So as they manufactured even more advanced weapons, they began to sell the older versions to other Spiders, making war the most profitable business for the GREY empire. During war, plenty of weaponry is sold, used and many are killed. This automatically helped to reduce the other problem that the GREY machine had - overpopulation. In war, instead of waiting for a few to die in the hospitals, the $\overline{ITS}$ could be wiped out and killed by the million!

The GREY machine also allowed $\overline{ITS}$ to choose a career, and so it became full of engineers, doctors, architects, scientists, mathematicians, etc. These $\overline{ITS}$ believed they were free, and would work to develop new technology and science.

As this was encouraged, great evolution happened in many fields: unwell $\overline{ITS}$ could have transplants; $\overline{ITS}$ who could not walk could run again; illnesses that were once incurable now had a cure; beautiful art and music was created: magnificent architectural and engineering achievements like flying machines and many other things were created.

But little did they know that all that lay in the womb of the surrogate mother was to be used as she pleased. From the discoveries on electromagnetism from the $\overline{IT}$ Tesla, the Spider monopolised electricity and sold it, instead of providing everyone with free renewable energy. From the same discoveries the Spider built a device that could command earthquakes and storms like magic and called it HAARP. The *discoveries on atomic power from* **ITS** *like Bohr, Curie and others were applied to manufacture more weapons instead of aiding medicine or the production energy. From the discoveries of* **IT** *Pasteur and those who followed the Spider created viruses and vaccinations to reduce overpopulation instead of making new cures for diseases. From the discoveries of biochemistry the Spider created pharmacology, banning plants and creating artificial substitutes that would create profit for the system.*

As the calendar wheel kept turning the Spider controlled **ITS** *by encouraging the use of legal substances that would help to keep the* **ITS** *asleep and numb. Any substance that could awaken the spirit of YOU or COLOURNESS or RAINBOWNESS was made illegal and scarce. The GREY machine allowed the illegal substances to be sold by gangs and mafias in the black markets for two purposes: one, to keep the minorities under a self-destructive addiction, and two, for them to have access to the substances and make some extra 'tax'-free cash.*

But the natural flow of the universe could not be stopped by the Gigantic Spider, and the Earth and the Universe came to a time of intergalactic shift, where the vibration of the Planet and all its inhabitants would change and no longer fit in the old GREY shoes. When this happen **ITS** *spontaneously started to remember they were once YOU and many got lost and overwhelmed by the fear of no longer being able to tolerate being an* **IT***. Those who found a way to navigate the reality of being a 'YOU' in the toxic womb of the Gigantic Spider, came to realise they were, in fact, COLOUR. But many, as they found their nature started fighting the Spider and made a lot of noise in the sticky threads of the Spider's web. The monster became angry and fought back with fury destroying, killing and annihilating the reputations of the fighters and using them as bait to show the other* **ITS** *what would happen if they woke up!*

But the shift could not be stopped and those who had not yet woken up started showing the symptoms of madness. Inside, their souls were screaming to them for COLOUR, but they lived so trapped in the illusion of GREY that they lost their minds and either killed themselves or were deemed clinically insane.

Those who survived didn't feel the need to fight back when they discovered they were COLOUR, started to remember that they were RAINBOW people. Instead, they experienced liberation inside and freedom from fear, because they knew there was no need to fight, and that simply by embracing their RAINBOWNESS again they would retrieve their Sovereignty and quietly slip through the threads of the big Spider web without being noticed.

As anarchy became imminent in the womb of the Spider and it started to crack and die, many saw the RAINBOW people sitting on the EARTH, breathing by themselves, safe, away from the Spider, and inspired, they found their way out before it was too late. The Spider eventually slipped into the ocean as a big ball of fire, drowning with her all ITS that were afraid to unplug themselves from the life support unit of the Gigantic GREY machine, afraid of being unable to breathe without her support. They stop breathing anyway as the Spider itself could no longer breathe.

Thanks to the evolution of science inside the womb of the Spider, many found enough proof to unplug themselves from the Spider and trust that they could be Sovereign reflections of the Light, breathing RAINBOW COLOURS.

The turning point of destiny for ITS was not only remembering their COLOURNESS or RAINBOWNESS, but to detach from anger, greed, depression, desire, and jealousy. Slowly and quietly by overcoming the fear of dying ITS would unplug from the Spider's life support machine. They would wrap their rainbow arms around their rainbow chest and close their rainbow eyes holding their breath as they fell back, slipping through the threads of the spider's web, falling into the arms of the real mother, the MOTHER INSIDE.

This story is being written as it is being read...

We handed over our sovereignty the day we became afraid of being ME, The day we became afraid of being COLOUR, RAINBOW, LIGHT. In that instant of fear, our independence and sovereignty as human beings, as inhabitants of Planet Earth were stolen in front of our eyes, and we let it happen. Why did we let it happen? Because we became afraid of death. When we lose our Spiritual Sovereignty we stop belonging, we stop breathing and being in union with the Self. We allow the Spider to become the surrogate mother that breathes for us.

We become afraid of our mortality and when we do that, we become afraid of living, surrendering our soul and our being to the GREY machine. What is that GREY machine in your own life? Banks? Wealth? War? TV? Government? Law? Cars?... **Can we bear the responsibility of being a sovereign human being**? Or do we care so little about our life that we allow a GREY machine to decide for us, think for us and control us?

What exactly will happen? I cannot answer that. But I do know for sure that violence will only create more violence, and fighting a machine that was born to fight and control as a Gigantic Spider does not seem wise. But starvation can make anything die. Stop feeding the machine! And maybe then a new story can be written by those who slip through the cracks.

> *"We are entering a period of human history that may provide an answer to the question of whether it is better to be smart than stupid. The most hopeful prospect is that the question will not be answered: if it receives a definite answer, that answer can only be that humans were a kind of "biological error", using their allotted 100,000 years to destroy themselves, and, in the process, much else. The species has surely developed the capacity to do just that, and a hypothetical extraterrestrial observer might well conclude that humans have demonstrated that capacity throughout their history, dramatically in the past few hundred years, with an assault on the environment that sustains life, on the diversity of more complex organisms, and with cold calculated savagery, on each other as well"*
>
> *(Noam Chomsky, 2003)*

"As soon as you're born they make you feel small,
By giving you no time instead of it all,
Till the pain is so big you feel nothing at all,
A working class hero is something to be,
A working class hero is something to be.

They hurt you at home and they hit you at school,
They hate you if you're clever and they despise a fool,
Till you're so fucking crazy you can't follow their rules,
A working class hero is something to be,
A working class hero is something to be.

When they've tortured and scared you for twenty odd years,
Then they expect you to pick a career,
When you can't really function you're so full of fear,
A working class hero is something to be,
A working class hero is something to be.

Keep you doped with religion and sex and TV,
And you think you're so clever and classless and free,
But you're still fucking peasants as far as I can see,
A working class hero is something to be,
A working class hero is something to be.

There's room at the top they are telling you still,
But first you must learn how to smile as you kill,
If you want to be like the folks on the hill,
A working class hero is something to be.
A working class hero is something to be.
If you want to be a hero well just follow me,
If you want to be a hero well just follow me".

~

"Power to the people, power to the people, power to the people…"
(John Lennon)

"4 Ahau
6 Ahau Katun concludes to allow 4 Ahau Katun
establish. This is the word that is in the essence
of its years according to the ancient names. Uucil
Yabnal, his-Seven-Waters, is the seat of 4 Ahau
Katun, in the Seven Waters of Chichen. Uac
Chuuahnal, Six-that-pours-pumpkins, in his face;
is at the South.

Dawn, Sunrise, will happen at the tail of Ah
Bococol, The-one-of narrow neck-who-pours-
vessels, but his face will be veiled; dead his look
will appear; crying for his bread, crying for his
water because devotions and reverence will be
denied. Trembling, trembling and dying will be its
power of lack of reverence from the Prince Lords,
from those who rule and govern. This is what 4
Ahau Katun, manifests: stinginess of bread, also
stinginess of water, obedience and respect will
subside because there is a different will and no
longer ever will be respected, because sweet it
was to its throat to receive respect but it will not
want to respect. Towards West it has its Mat and
its Throne; sudden death will be its essence. Then
will be Batabes, Those-of-the-axe, foreigners and
up-starters that will choke by the neck the Halach
Uiniques, Leaders of the towns, making them
vomit blood. This is the essence of the katun."
(Chilam Balam)

Chapter VIII
Health Sovereignty

Our Sovereignty cannot be fully retrieved until we explore the realms of health and well-being. To be able to do this we need to include our physical, emotional and intellectual body and 'mind' or 'spirit'. Let's review different meanings attached to the word Health:

H E A L T H
Derived from the Proto-Indo-European 'kailo', meaning whole, uninjured, of good omen.
From the Latin 'salus' or 'salutis', meaning prosperity, good wish, safety.
From the Latin 'salutaris', meaning healthful, health-giving, wholesome, beneficial, saving.
From the Latin 'medella', meaning cure, remedial treatment; healing, healing power.

The general condition of your body.
Wholeness; being whole, sound or well.
Free from illness, the state of being well.

We could possibly summarise health as an experience of:

WHOLENESS

Together with the loss of Socio-Political-Economic Sovereignty, we lost our Health Sovereignty at the hands of the Gigantic GREY Spider. Today the notion of health has been reduced to the absence of illness by using as many preventive drugs as possible and by chopping and cutting the ill bits out of the body. A medical doctor is not required to know about emotional, intellectual or spiritual balance. In general, most of our western medicine focuses simply on treating organs and limbs. In many cases, practitioners do not seem to take into consideration that the skin full of water sitting in front of them is a human being.

I still recall, as if it were yesterday, the talk Don Mariano gave us as we started our first year in medical school in Universidad La Salle, Mexico city. I was so full of enthusiasm and excitement, feeling that I was fulfilling my destiny, as well as going against the recommendation of the LC religious (what is this? Can we spell it out?) to join the order and follow my vocation serving god and people. Little did I know at the time how my life was going to transform and how enrolling in medical school was one of the foundation stones that would serve as a catalyst for that change.

On that first day, Don Mariano spoke with passion and strength coming from the depths of his being. I believe very few people took him seriously because he was an old brother from the order that founded the school of medicine. Young people often dismiss and even despise elders. As we lost respect for life we lost respect for those who remind us that life is not eternal. In those days of my early education you could see how that infection was well spreading through the young generation.

At some point in his speech he used words that I recall like this:

> "*...the medical doctor that stops believing in a greater source than him or herself, has lost his path and must stop practicing, because he has forgotten he is only human, just as his or her patients...*"

As I was a 'spiritual believer', I always knew inside that there was a greater source of creation, so my heart jumped and resonated with the words I had just heard. I was trying to reconcile inside me the reality of Spirit and my pursuit of medical science and his words inspired me to continue my journey and have hope that one day I would be able to put at rest my dilemma. In his tone I also heard a warning, almost as if he was trying to communicate non-verbally the dangers of the profession. To my surprise it didn't take long for me to prove that my intuition was correct. He was letting us know what was ahead and what could happen to us.

In the first year or medical training, anatomy is one of the priorities and we had to dissect human bodies. We worked in groups and each group had its own 'subject' ready for dissection in a freezer. We also had to do dissections on bodies that were recently deceased, and for that purpose we had to attend the morgue on a regular basis to participate in autopsies and work on dissections corresponding to whatever chapter we happened to be studying at the time.

We had to become numb to the smell of both fresh and stale blood and, something I could never do, have our lunch as the autopsy was being performed.

Sometimes we had to wait for hours until a body came into the morgue. A human being had to die so we could practice. We knew that when it was payday in the area, we would get more practice because on those days people go out, lose control and drink too much, leading to fatal accidents. More fresh bodies for us on the metal planks,-, it also meant to become familiar with music playing in the rooms where the bodies are kept, become numb to the smell of stale blood and formol and, the one I could never overcome, to have your lunch as the autopsy was being performed. It's a surreal experience to wait for someone to die so you can get your homework done. It's an experience that is difficult, almost impossible, to explain.
One day we were waiting at the morgue. This was not a payday so there were no fresh bodies in the morgue.

After a long wait we decided to go outside to get some fresh air. As we were chatting away in our white coats a couple approached the building and sat down on a bench right beside us. A few moments later, one of our colleagues came running out and shouted with excitement: "there's a body here finally! Let's finish and go home!" As we joined the excitement I looked over at to the couple sitting on the bench. They were the grief-stricken parents of the man whose body we were going to work on. I never felt so much shame in my life. They looked at us in tears and despair. I can still feel their look penetrating my soul saying "how dare you!"

After that day I knew what Don Mariano meant and I knew in my heart if that numbness is what it takes to reconcile Spirit and science, then I wasn't interested. That type of "science" was killing my Spirit, devouring me without me even noticing it, making me unfeeling and dismissive of human pain.

That day I saw my ignorance as big as it could get. I might as well have killed the man with my own hands. In that moment I was blind and deaf to the world around me. I was no longer ME I was an $\overline{IT}$ working for the big GREY Spider, looking for approval and validation of my being through an acceptable and valid science, believing that the letters M.D. would define who I was meant to be and give me credibility to speak MY VOICE.

The GREY machine had successfully $\overline{IT}$-alise me. I could no longer see human beings. All I saw were piles of flesh, fat and blood to experiment on. I no longer saw RAINBOW people, because I failed to see part of myself or ME in those poor people sitting on the bench. I did not see ME crying, but rather $\overline{ITS}$, a 'mother' and a 'father.' At the cold metal table in the morgue I no longer recognised ME. I could only see a fresh body for the first year students to practice on before it became too cold to be of any more use to us.

I always have to remind myself that this was only first year. More difficult challenges were to come when, instead of learning about anatomy, one had to learn about physiology which means to understand how the human body functions when it is alive.

One would have to wonder, if this is the basic of all medical training, is it similar for those who study the 'human mind' in psychiatry? Is the mind reduced to a bunch of neurotransmitters working inside a big grey mass called the brain?

I think it's fair to ask you, the reader: Would you trust the information you are hearing from me more if I had the letters M.D. after my name? Would this book suddenly become more valid to YOU? Or would it suddenly become irrelevant to YOU? In general, the majority of people would consider it more valid because we have been conditioned that way. We associate expertise and credibility with titles and initials after a name. Once again the GREY machine has worked to perfection in making us $\overline{ITS}$ that have importance or position in society because of letters beside more letters. We no longer see 'human beings,' we see 'letters' and titles.

This impersonal way of thinking and living has spread like a pandemic virus, cutting us off from the true self in every manifestation of life; cutting us off from the essence and 'spirit' of things and beings. In the same manner the letters:

m e d i c a l   d o c t o r

are cut off from any experience of wholeness and well-being. They are initials that give permission to human beings to be right no matter what, and therefore grant power and authority with little regard to the ethical values of the person.

So what combination of letters do you need to see to give validity to the information you believe in?

Your answer to that question will give you an insight into how much power the GREY machine has over you, and how much of your sovereignty has been lost. Most of the population of ITS have lost their capacity to trust themselves; to think for themselves; to speak for themselves and to breathe for themselves. They need big letters to speak for them and tell them what to believe and what to trust. We have numbed our intuition.

As everything has an origin and a story behind it, it would be interesting to explore what is behind the western practice of medicine. For that purpose I would like to introduce you to the man considered to be the "father" of western medicine - the great Greek physician Hippocrates Asclepiads (Kos, Greece, 460-377? BCE).

Interestingly, there is no "mother" of western medicine, just as there is no feminine essence, energy or figure in most western religious systems, or socio-political-economic systems, but we will deal with that later.

Hippocrates learned medicine from his father Heracleides, as he came from a family of physicians, and from the Asklepieion in Kos (healing temples dedicated to Asklepius). He is best known for having separated medicine from spirituality or, in western words, he separated 'true science' from 'superstition' and 'magic'. He introduced the belief that illness was not a punishment from the gods but that it was the result of natural and physical causes in the person's body and its environment. When the four humors of the body (blood, black bile, yellow bile and phlegm) were out of balance the person would become ill. He observed that illness had a crisis stage, after which it would subside and stop or increase, leading to death. In years to come, this understanding of the natural dance of the body regaining balance would be the starting point for homeopathic treatment.

Hippocrates dedicated his life to observing and treating illness, keeping records of all the methods used and their effects. These records, essays, research and the classifications Hippocrates and his students gave to illness diagnosis, treatment and prognosis, became the *Hippocratic Corpus*, giving birth to clinical medicine.

Hippocrates was also named Asclepiades after Asclepius, the Greek god of medicine, son of the god Apollo and Coronis. The myth of Asclepius is the ground on which Hippocrates and his physician ancestors walked. When we recall the mythology behind the story we can understand the essence that permeates our lives as human beings. Mythology becomes the canvas, or collective unconscious, in which we paint the individual stories of the human race. The myth of Asclepius is the canvas upon which western medicine was painted.

Coronis, Asclepius' mother, was made pregnant by Apollo and during her pregnancy she fell in love with another human. Enraged by this, Apollo sent his twin sister Artemis (the Roman goddess Diana) to kill Coronis. As her body was burning on a funeral pyre, Apollo felt guilty for killing his unborn child. He cut open Coronis' womb and rescued his son. Some suggest that this story explains the son's name, as Asclepius is understood to mean 'to cut open'. Apollo gave Asclepius into the care of the Centaur Cheiron, son of the god Cronos (Saturn).

The Centaurs were known for their unruly behaviour but Cheiron was an exception, being kind and well educated in music, hunting, archery and healing.. He was always one step ahead and he taught many heroes including Jason, Achilles, Herakles and Asclepius, the arts of hunting and healing.

On his wedding, King Pirithous of the Lapiths decided to invite the Centaurs to the celebration and as usually happened after drinking wine, upheaval broke loose between the Centaurs and the Lapiths. Herakles (Hercules), draw his bow and started shooting arrows to stop the Centaurs, he had dipped his arrows in the venom of Hydra, the most savage and lethal of all snakes. As Cheiron intervened in the scene trying to pacify the upheaval, Herakles shot his most poisonous arrow, hitting the body of his master, the Centaur Cheiron.

The poison created a painful wound that Cheiron would have to endure trough immortality. It is said that Cheiron eventually exchanged his immortality for a mortal death, taking Prometeus place in Mount Caucasus, and in that manner ending the pain he had to endure. Cheiron was placed in the sky after his death forming the constellation of Sagittarius.

As Asclepius learned the art of healing and medicine from Cheiron he became a very skilled healer, curing people from various illnesses. It is said that Athena gave Asclepius some Gorgon blood – the Gorgons were female creatures that had snakes for hair and one gaze of their eyes could turn a human into stone. It was well known that the blood from a Gorgon's right side could bring the dead back to life. Whether Asclepius used the blood or his skills to bring the dead back to life we do not know for sure, but as he challenged human mortality and broke the natural balance of life, he upset Hades the god of the underworld and worried Zeus as a world of immortal beings would bring chaos and disharmony to Gaia (Earth). That was why, on the insistence of Hades, Zeus fired a thunderbolt that brought Asclepius to his tragic death.

Asclepius was always depicted with a rod and a snake roped around it. This was the symbol of a healer in those times, as many of the illnesses were products of parasitic worms and these were pulled out of the person's skin by making an incision in front of its path and winding it on a stick. Also snake bites were lethal and the rod also symbolised that a person had the skill to cure snake bites. Another common association was that serpents are known to die and be reborn, to shed their skin and renew themselves, and from ancient times this natural capacity of the animal was a source of inspiration in healing myths and symbols. It is interesting that the figure of Moses in ancient Egypt was also depicted with a rod and a snake, or snake staff, according to the book of Exodus, a different story from that of Asclepius, but the symbol of the snake and the staff makes itself present through Moses in Egypt around the 14th century $_{BCE}$.

Today this symbol is still used by most medical organisations, just as Asclepius rests in the sky as the constellation of Ophiuchus "the serpent barer."

When we observe today's medical system and the mythology that informed its creation two interesting analogies stand out related to the way we are born and to the way we die.

In the myth of Asclepius he is pulled out of the burning body of his mother when Apollo cut open her womb to rescue him. In today's world we can see humans incubating in the womb of our 'death mother' Gaia, the Earth that has been killed because its children wanted more. The Earth has been sacrificed in the hands of greed. We diminish her resources and use her at our ignorant will. Just like Asclepius, we are born of a mother that has no apparent life and is burning in a funeral pyre of oil wells and weapons, suffocating from the combustion of fuels.

The medical profession, skilled like Apollo, cuts open the womb of the mother to pull us out in the millions of caesarean births that are well planned and scheduled throughout the planet. In that way our arrival into Earth ceases to be a natural and organic entry that will prepare us for life, and is instead an artificial entry that disconnects us from life. There is no connection with the mother Gaia as a breathing being. To our eyes she is death, inert matter, and there is no connection with the mother at birth, as in the majority of cases the mother is asleep or numb during birth. This loss of connection with the very source of life, the 'mother', will inform the rest of our lives as separate individuals and leave a memory of disconnection, aloneness, emptiness and its corresponding craving for union, wholeness and connection.

Then as we become skilled in the art of medical practice and we learn that death can be delayed, we bring the dead back into life, just like Asclepius. We challenge the natural order of life, upsetting the lords of the underworld and death. Our medical practices and social behaviour are orientated to conquer death, not by seeing it as a transformative experience but by denying its existence. Our medical profession sees death as a failure and at all costs it is to be avoided, reversed, and denied, and life is to be prolonged by every single artificial and technological means possible. When we deny death, we disconnect ourselves from the natural impermanent nature of the Universe and consciousness; we disconnect ourselves from understanding that aging and death are a natural part of life and a beautiful and essential part of the journey of human existence.

So through medicine, our entry into human existence is artificially controlled by the big GREY machine's physicians and so is our exit.

If you want to know what a culture or a society has become simply observe how its people are born and how they die. It is at the entry and the exit of humanness that we are taught how to live and how to respect life. Both experiences are the in-breath and out-breath of death. They are the shedding of the skin, just like the snake. In the entry (birth) we abandon a non-material existence and enter into a material world, and in the exit (death) we shed the material robes to re-enter a non-material existence. These are the moments where we experience cosmic union and cosmic separation, the breathing dance that has existed since the beginning and that will play itself out until the end, only to start again in the eternal cycle of creation.

In these important transitions where we are going through the shedding, the fear of leaving a life behind and entering an apparent unknown experience, when we most need to be conscious, in our society we are provided with drugs to numb the pain and make us unconscious to what is happening. As soon as we are born we are rushed into a box, one which will contain us and teach us that life is about finding boxes, buying boxes and fitting into boxes, and as soon as we die we are rushed into the box that will keep our rotten remains under the soil, occupying space in the Earth even after we are dead.

In this way we could very easily say, based on our entry (birth) and exit (death) that our life on Earth is about:

NUMBING PAIN AND FITTING INTO BOXES

After Hippocrates split medicine off from superstition and magic, after 'science' and 'Spirit' became separate matters, Aristotle (Stageira, Greece, 384-322$_{BCE}$) introduced rational, logical thinking, giving us another piece of the puzzle that would contribute greatly to the origins of biological psychiatry. Plato (Athens?, Greece, 428-348$_{BCE}$), established that there are two different types of mental disorder: "divinely inspired" and "physically caused." In the first one, the person received prophetic and mystic powers and in the other the person lost psychic balance and the capacity to behave in an appropriate manner.

Aristotle, Plato's disciple, then gave the final cut to any relationship between Spirit and science, stating that there was only one cause for mental disorders: a physical cause.

From then onwards medical science has evolved, developing and growing, inside of the womb of the Spider, artificially disconnected from the very source of human life, Planet Earth and Spirit, 'the Breath'. Our understanding of real and true became so far removed from the story of creation, where all was simply a beam of Light breathing rainbow colours into material forms that we came to reduce human beings to anatomy, biology and physiology.

This helped greatly in the process of 'YOU' becoming $\overline{\text{I}}$-alised, because a human being, once an independent manifestation of the divine, was now reduced to a body full of water, organs and neurotransmitters that could be studied and fixed like a machine. We became our own projects and objects of study, making the absolute truth only that which can be measured and observed by human eyes behind microscopes.

The centre of humanness and being alive became the vital organs such as the heart and lungs, allowing physicians to declare a body dead as soon as these organs failed to do their work, as soon as they organs stopped breathing and pulsing.

Later, physicians realised that the heart and lungs were not necessarily at the driving seat of the human body, but rather the brain.

Now, physicians do not declare a body dead when the heart or lungs stop, they have to wait for the brain to stop. In the course of medical evolution, amazing machines have been created that can work as surrogate lungs and heart, keeping the body biologically alive until doctors decide it is time to die. The lucky ones, like Asclepius did, are brought back to life. Always denying death and dying and making an artificial intervention in the natural entry into humanness, our birth, and the natural exit from humanness, our death.

Medical science has achieved miracles worthy of our admiration and honour and I myself bow at our capacity to evolve scientifically and technologically to help people regain quality of life or become functional again. It is admirable the tasks and achievements that some branches of the medical profession have taken and how they have organically evolved towards facilitating life and well-being, providing an experience of

WHOLENESS

However, unfortunately, the majority of western medical science is focused today on developing:

DRUGS THAT FIX PAIN

With the establishment of the pharmaceutical industry, all of the wise voices from the Earth - its plants, harmonious living and natural balance - were successfully forgotten as magic fixes were introduced to make pain disappear. The Earth and its products have been gradually banned because they impact profits. Why? Because plants and herbal remedies don't have the same side effects as the 'magic pills' and in many cases they provide a permanent cure for the illness, and people no longer need drugs.

Permanent cures are not good for business. What is good for business is that the pharmaceutical solution fails more that it succeeds in order to create a recurrent flow of customers and a steady market. Again, greed becomes the engine that puts in motion the institutionalisation of 'The Health System', no different from the religious, political, economic and social institutions. In this model of Health, illness is necessary to create a market that requires the services and products that the industry provides.

ILLNESS is what makes the HEALTH INDUSTRY possible, WHOLENESS and WELL-BEING are a threat to it.

Once the pharmaceutical industry dug its teeth into the profession of healing and medicine controlled it with its venomous poison of greed, very little of the traditional ways of healing and medicine were left. We became the children of 'pain killers' where health means:

KILL, CUT OR AMPUTATE PAIN

The reason for the pain, its cause, its source, are no longer relevant. What matters most is:

DO NOT FEEL THE PAIN

As far as our map of the human being continues to be based on the archaic understanding that a human being is made simply of anatomy, biology and physiology, we are truncating any possibility for evolution in medical science, as all we can become is more technologically efficient and chemically sophisticated to ensure more effective and efficient:

DO NOT FEEL THE PAIN

This tunnel vision of the human being is also the canvas upon which the science of studying the human mind was painted. Psychiatry evolved as the branch of medical practice that studied the abnormal behaviours of human beings. From the contributions of many great minds psychology evolved and, with it, psychotherapy and many different counselling practices.

In its origins, the practice of mental health was dedicated to observing, diagnosing and treating human beings that presented abnormal behaviour in **'asylums for the imbeciles.'** Today, 20 centuries after the first asylums were created, all that has changed is that we no longer call them 'asylums' but **'psychiatric hospitals,'** and it's not politically correct to call human beings 'imbeciles' so we call them **'mentally ill'**. But the essential understanding of 'mental illness' has not evolved very much, apart from having more sophisticated, descriptive manuals with names for every illness and behaviour, and more access to chemicals that can sedate the 'patient' with fewer side effects than before.

Over the years, highly unethical practices were (and still are) taking place in the 21st century in modernised and sanitised **'psychiatric hospitals',** where human beings were Lobotomized and/or Electrocuted with ECT (Electroconvulsive Therapy). In 1949 we gave the Nobel Prize to Dr. Antonio Egaz Moniz, for his discovery of the therapeutic value of leucotomy in certain types of psychoses (lobotomy- performed on the frontal lobe of the brain).

Today, mental illness still cannot be diagnosed by any other means than ticking boxes from a list of abnormal and maladaptive behaviours and their frequency. The pathology of mental illness is reduced to studying the effects of neurotransmitters (dopamine, serotonin, etc.) in the brain. The medication prescribed only regulates neurotransmitters; it does not bring wellbeing to the person neither cure them. Biological psychiatry cannot explain the causes of this maladaptive behaviour, so we simply administer tranquilizers of many different kinds and shapes to sedate the people presenting the unwanted behaviour.

The criteria defining normal and abnormal behaviour is set by the person doing the assessment and diagnosis. What does this mean? If you laugh a tone too loud you are no longer joyful but manic? If you cry a tear too many you are no longer grieving but depressed? If you hear a voice too many you are no longer a mystic but schizophrenic? It all depends on who you talk to and if that laugh, that tear or that voice is too much for is the particular person that is listening to you, then your behaviour is abnormal and maladaptive; you will be labelled as an unstable human being.

I remember when I first came to Ireland I was referred to as manic because we are relatively loud in Mexico. And when some of my family visited Ireland they perceived Irish people as depressed! So where is the boundary, I ask? Even culture can make us judge a human being as too loud, too sad, too quiet, too happy only because they are different. Imagine if you are not a friend or family but the therapist or psychiatrist in front of this person? A Mexican in Ireland can present plenty of abnormal and maladaptive behaviour just as the Irish would in Mexico. So what defines the boundary that earns you the label 'mentally ill'? This example only considers something as simple as a cultural difference; imagine what happens when you add: family upbringing, education, religion, language, political orientation, birth, trauma,...When you simply add LIFE!

We all have the capacity for madness; we are all receptors of the universal consciousness and we all have an individual and a collective story that channels through our body. This body and being, when exposed to extreme circumstances, is capable of anything, ordinary people have walked into a flaming building to rescue another human being, ordinary people have pulled out a gun to kill. We all have the capacity to be 'the hero' and we all have the capacity to be 'the murderer'.

Most people don't want to hear this because it's inconvenient and uncomfortable to consider that perhaps the human beings in 'psychiatric hospitals' are not separate, mentally ill beings. Perhaps they are just like us, going though grieving, anger, or trauma. Perhaps they are simply human beings that are too sensitive and alive to tolerate the unhealthy and disharmonious noise that our world makes as we feed the Gigantic GREY Spider with fear and greed.

These sensitive human beings are the barometers of society and in times when we were connected to the Universe and the Earth these human beings were our healers and guides, our shamans and medicine people.

If you are ever curious to know how well we are doing as a society, pay a visit to a psychiatric ward and have a chat with any of the amazing human beings there when they are not sedated. Then you will really have an insight into how our society looks and how the demons of greed and fear have devoured Planet Earth and us.

As long as we live under our conditioned fear of pain, illness, aging and death; as long as we need 'pain killers' to be and live, the establishment will hold on to our Health Sovereignty.

In the moment that you overcome the fear of pain, illness, aging and death, all natural elements of a human life, then you will retrieve your:
WHOLE SOVEREIGNTY

There was a time before Aristotle, before the father of medicine Hippocrates, before Asclepius, when human beings knew they were RAINBOW people and lived as one with the WHOLE Universe, with the WHOLE of Gaia, and with the WHOLE of their COLOURNESS.

There was a time when the absolute reality was that of union and oneness, and the relative reality was the illusion of separation. Respect for the Planet and its resources was a given because there were no mountains but only ME experiencing the world as a mountain, there were no oceans but only ME experiencing the world as an ocean, there was no darkness but only ME experiencing the absence of light, there was no light but only ME experiencing emptiness.

All was, and still is, an extension of the one self, just as alchemy explains that there was, and still is, only one 'mind'.   Hermes

Trimegistrus (Greece - Mercury in Rome – Imhotep in Egypt), was associated with magic and what we know today as alchemy. The Emerald Tablet accredited to Hermes seems to date back to 3000_{BCE}. The symbol depicted with him was formed by two snakes entwined in single rod crowned by feathers/wings, commonly known as the caduceus. This symbol is used today by medical institutions sometimes confused as the Rod of Asclepius.

 The caduceus, the herald's staff, speaks volumes about the myth of creation and life, the one centre piece supporting life, the two serpents making creation possible and the mystical connection crowned by feathers. The symbol of feathered snakes can be traced to almost all indigenous wisdoms around the Planet. In all traditions it is a deity that generally embodies wisdom, life and death and brings the balance of the polar opposites, the feminine and the masculine, the earth and the sky, the humanness as separation and the union of all at the crown. In Mesoamerican mythology Quetzalcoatl embodies the feathered snake appearing in many of the stone carvings and temples as a main deity.

Before our western indoctrination, mostly evolving from Greece and Rome, we can trace many different practices of medicine and well-being that, in their essence, just like Alchemy, emerged from Spirit. These were well documented methods of restoring balance in the human body from a perspective of WHOLENESS, understanding that the human incarnation consisted of many layers and energies, gross and subtle. If these were out of balance they would manifest as disharmony in the person's body(physical), emotions (astral) and intellect (causal).

Among these practices we can trace around the 8th century $_{BCE}$ in China the 'I Ching' or 'Book of Changes' from which Traditional Chinese Medicine has evolved is still practiced to this day. In the North and North West of what is now India, we find the Vedic civilization and their texts, the Rigvedas, in the 10th century BC, which would become the basis of Ayurvedic medicine, also successfully practiced to this day.

There are no perfect times in human history, and it is not about idealising one philosophy or another, but it is about questioning what we consider in our lives as true and immovable. When we stop asking questions we become stagnant and stop evolving. Medical science today does not have all the answers, it has only one more piece of the great puzzle that the human being and life is.

I see that if we are to reunite Health and Wholeness, medical science needs to reconnect to 'Spirit', to the 'mother'. We need to learn from the immense wisdom of indigenous people and their knowledge of plants and Spirit, together with the incredible and sophisticated technological knowledge of western medicine.

In all of the ancient practices exists a mother of medicine, the Earth, as the source of all we need to survive. It is the *'mother'* the Earth, who provides nourishment; learning to read the *sacred texts* of *'father'* Sky is then what complements the method and formula of harmonious living, health, and wholeness.

The practices emerged from indigenous wisdom, from living and being in harmony with the Earth where we live. These people are YOU and ME. We are the descendants of the indigenous people who walked the Earth 3000 - 5000 years ago and before that. Indigenous wisdom and its healing art is accessible to anyone who is willing to take the risk of being Sovereign, because it means to fully embrace the Whole of your being understanding that the society, the economy and the politics that exist are simply a projection of the inner self; understanding that there is no 'god' outside yourself to whom you pray for forgiveness or fortune; but that there is only YOU, the one consciousness, the one mind experiencing itself in thousand-fold forms and states of being.

To reclaim the whole of your Sovereignty means to trust yourself and to unconditionally accept who you are in compassionate understanding of the limitations caused by ignorance.
To completely become a Sovereign human being you have to accept responsibility for your physical, your emotional and your intellectual body and 'mind' (Spirit). You are responsible for your physicality,

you are responsible for your emotional reactions and you are responsible for your thoughts. There is nobody to blame, only you in charge of your life and well-being.

This is how the game becomes simple, and how, suddenly, when there is no one to blame, suffering ceases as it cannot attach pain to anything or anyone but the self. As suffering ceases, the self can regain its crystal clear awareness and vision and it stops being deafened by fear. From this state of being we can experience mystical union with the LIGHT and embrace RAINBOWNESS, not as a concept of pseudo-spirituality, but as the expression of our true self, becoming the embodiment of the Awakened Mind.

"Truth! Certainty!
That in which there is no doubt!
That which is above is from that which is
below, and that which is below is from
that which is above, working the miracles
of one.
As all things were from one.
It's father the Sun and
its mother the Moon.
The Earth carried in her belly
and the Wind nourished it in her belly
as Earth which shall become Fire.
Feed the Earth from that which is subtle,
with the greatest power.
It ascends from the earth to the heaven
and becomes ruler over that which is
above and that which is below.
And I have already explained the meaning
of the whole of this in two of these books
of mine."
(Emerald Tablet, Hermes Trimegistrus)

Chapter IX
Voices of Science

The Dream of 'The One'

Log 13.2.1.4.3/2053$_{CE}$

We are the survivors of a human race that once inhabited 'blue-dot 44' planet of a remote solar system in a bare spiral galaxy that we called the Milky Way, known in outer space as '@' (serpent galaxy).

After the calendar marked 13.0.0.0.0 we lived 20 years of gradual collapse of our socio-political-economic systems and religions. The masses were lost in fear and despair, I was just a kid. The crumbling governments tried to join a terrified humanity in one unified system called Earth United (EU), as they disclosed to the public that there were other intelligent beings living in space that had been in close relationship with humans for centuries.

But as the systems collapsed and we experienced scarcity and famine, fear took hold of humanity and the broken machine we were at the time could not endure the change, all causing more damage than good.

Food and water were scarce and many were dying of starvation which led to the brutal War of Wars (WW). This war prolonged for another 20 years, and we did horrendous things to each other. In this war more than humans were involved, each side fighting for the same objective, to control the weakest link. The use of strange nuclear and viral weapons devastated all that was left on the planet, leaving it dry like a desert of rock and silence, clouding the sun and making it cold. A few of us managed to survive as we were helped by other translucent beings that shined a RAINBOW light.

Now the war is over and as there is nothing left on Earth the prognosis for survival of our species is low.

Log 13.2.1.4.4/2053$_{CE}$

These translucent beings are teaching us how to grow crops and plants out of dry rocks; they are helping us to manifest water, which I have a great difficulty with because it evaporates as soon as I want to drink it. And they keep helping us to remember how life was before this disaster took place.

We are trying to remember what went wrong and what happened that we could not manage to change without violence. These RAINBOW beings are recording my entries in a holographic image that translates itself into numbers and geometrical shapes and then gets absorbed by a fountain of white 'soma' as they call it. I have never seen technology like it, but it reminds me of the games I used to play when I was a child. I was born with the century and in those times all we did was to play on computers and x-boxes against zombies and aliens. I spent my childhood pretending I was fighting in wars and killing thousands. I knew how to load a machine gun, how to fire missiles and how to cut the scalp off my enemies. Little did I know that I was going to spend my adult life trapped inside one of those war video games, only this time the dead were not standing up again and you could smell the blood and feel the pain of every wound.

Tomorrow I am going to be put into trance by some of these beings to recall what happened to us. This being that calls itself Lucia is always with me and she has explained that in order to evolve we need to recall our history as a human race. Apparently we have to understand clearly how we lived and the decisions we made before we can change and form a new society. Lucia has explained that if we do not make the effort to remember the story of human beings even before we were born then all that information will play in the background like a computer programme unconsciously making us choose the same paths we chose before leading us only to more violence.

Log 13.2.1.4.5/2053CE

Entry: Lucia:
Human subject in trance and stable; deep and relaxed breathing. Human will narrate visions as they happen. Starting time: Sun 3'1/2.

Entry: Subject:
I feel my body getting warm; I can feel a white mist around me, like fresh air. It feels as if I have a lot space to breathe. I can see a bright tunnel revolving in front of me, I am walking into the tunnel, it is changing colour and shape, revolving faster. Something is pulling me into it. I am travelling very fast trough the tunnel. Bright lights, twists and turns, still travelling.

All has stopped now.

An image is becoming clear around me, I am floating, I am floating above the Earth, all seems quiet. Blue and green shades make the landscape of mountains and oceans.

I can see a large stone construction. Pumapunku. The visual of the surroundings is breathtaking and the construction is impeccable. I see RAINBOW beings walking up and down the pyramid-like structures. At the top of these structures I can see big spheres of light becoming brighter and fading away, as if they are 'star-gates' transporting beings in and out. Time is 17,000 calendar cycles before today. 'Blue-dot 44' was a rare combination of sophisticated and complex forms of biological life in evolution. These beings come here to learn about life.

Time is passing fast, the landscape is changing fast.
The Sun does not rise in the same place, the Earth has shifted.
I am still above Pumapunku. I can see human beings in it now.
It is amazing!

I am moving. I am flying above the Earth and seeing many civilizations of archaic human-like beings talking to rainbow people and living harmoniously with the Earth. They chant,

141

dance and live in the same manner all over the world, the only difference is how they communicate with each other.

In each of these communities there is a Tree of Life, 'Tule' who speaks to them about creation and the wisdom of the ancestors. I can even hear its whispers on the wind.

Time is moving, it is now 6,000 calendar cycles before today. Settlements of human-like beings unfold around Mesopotamia, Egypt, Indus Valley, Shang, Mesoamerica and Andean South America. Culture and civilization starts showing its face on the planet. Amazing structures are built and complex social orders develop, many of these humans in close communication with RAINBOW beings and other intelligent forms from outer space.

Some groups become stronger and, infected by greed, start conquering their neighbours. Harmony is no longer the ruler of the planet. Now at the throne Greed and Desire have become rulers.

It is now 3,000 calendar cycles BEFORE today and there are no longer civilizations but empires. Most of the activity is concentrated around large clusters of buildings and the population seems to gravitate to those empire clusters. As time moves on, these empires commence to dictate social, political, economical and religious rules.

Some human beings far away from these clusters are able to remain connected to their traditions and wisdom but most of those living inside the clusters or under the rule of one or another empire receive indoctrination about the way they should behave and the way they should live.

Some spread the belief that the Earth was flat. Many followed without questioning.

As time went by the natural cycles of the Sun and the Moon started getting lost and, in their place, artificial counts of time were imposed. These disconcerted the human psyche a great deal as the rhythm of everyday living became gradually more and more disconnected from the natural cycles of the planet, from our mother, The Earth and life became an artificial routine. Most clusters never spoke to their Tree of Life again; 'Tule' was never important to the empires, it was simply dry wood.

As we lost connection from the cycles of the Universe and became part of artificial cycles we lost contact with the essence of interconnection and we started to believe that we were all separate individuals. We took joy and pride in war and conquest and as leisure we developed games that would involve violence and public torture. The poison of Greed was running through our veins and it found its brother Fear which became the perfect police man of order and peace.

Religions were created to unite humans in one belief and in the name of that truth war and murder were made necessary around the planet.

A few became rich and powerful and the masses became poor and fearful.

There was no end to the expansion of the empires. They only changed names and rulers but they kept spreading their clusters and beliefs further and further, killing all that they encountered, engulfing the smaller clusters, never satisfied, never content.

Some believed that the Earth was at the centre of the Universe. And many followed without questioning.

It is now only 500 calendar cycles before today. Some voices started speaking to the empires about the ancient understanding that the Earth was not at the centre, but rather the Sun, although this time they had mathematical proof and by the use of the telescope this could finally be confirmed, but the empire silenced and imprisoned those who dared challenge the commonly accepted truth.

I am confused, what was the need to suppress the understanding that the Earth was not at the centre of the Universe? It was common sense; all ancient calendars take into account cycles of remote stars and planets, how come after all these years of evolution we decided to regress to such a limited perspective of reality? I cannot understand why? Why we did not listen? What was so wrong in questioning information that was misrepresenting reality?! Could you not see there were beings from outer space on Earth before us, and with us, we always knew the Earth was not at the centre of the Universe! I knew that from the moment I was born!

Entry: Lucia:
Subject showing signs of distress. Up frequency 1.2Hz.
Subject stable.

This was to become the template for the next 500 cycles; every time voices spoke about different truths we dismissed them, and empires just kept getting bigger and more controlling.

The art of technology and science evolved rapidly and in the 100 cycles that preceded 13.0.0.0.0, we were able to scientifically prove and confidently understand that:

❖ *The Sun, although the centre of our Solar System, was just one more star among the many billions of stars that formed our galaxy.*

❖ *Our galaxy was only one of billions of observable galaxies.*

❖ *The beginning of the Universe, contrary to the big-bang theory, was manifested by a surplus of particles of matter from antimatter. We understood this to be fundamental to the existence of matter.*

❖ *Gravity was not a constant but a variable factor as remote galaxies picked up speed instead of slowing down as they become more distant from one another and as there was more accountable gravitational force than matter in the Universe.*

❖ *Empty space was not empty as even in ZPF (zero-point field) positive values of energy could be obtained.*

❖ *Organisms were formed by cells. Cells were formed by molecules. Molecules were formed by atoms.*

❖ *Atoms were formed fundamentally but not exclusively by:*
• *Atomic particles-Nuclei of protons and neutrons with a cloud of electrons orbiting in different patterns around it and the hypothetical Higgs boson.*
• *Subatomic particles-Quarks, Leptons and Bosons.*

❖ *Isotopes were atoms with a different mass, containing a different number of neutrons and the same number of protons, which led us to understand and use radioactivity.*

❖ *The number of protons determined which type of element the atom represented.*

❖ *Electromagnetism was the natural force that resulted from the interaction of electrical charged particles. A natural field of energy surrounding all matter.*

❖ *All fundamental sub-atomic particles were simply strings of energy vibrating at a different frequency. This meant that particles were both material and a wave of energy operating outside TIME and three- dimensional space.*

❖ *Particles had the capacity to entangle with one another once they had been in close contact, responding accordingly with the particle they are entangled with.*

❖ *We knew that an atom of Hydrogen was composed by one proton and one electron.*

❖ *Particles, although behaving with uncertainty, follow symmetric patterns.*

❖ *The same ratios observed in the behaviour of particles could be identified in the configuration of galaxies and the unfolding universe.*

❖ *The observer affected the result of the observation as once the intent of an experiment was set, even if the experiment was cancelled, results were obtained...*

I cannot believe this! Before I was born we had all the information we needed to understand that matter was not really solid but only the waves of possibilities that manifested at the will of the observer. Clearly this explained that the world around us was not solid although it appeared solid. We knew about frequencies of vibration and light spectrums and how shifts of vibration created different shapes and forms. We were able to heal one another with intention and conducing energy. Free and sustainable resources were always accessible to all but we let greed make us dependent on our archaic system of electrical power and combustion fuel energy. We had the technology to amplify the harmonious vibration of the Earth and with it our own vibration, but our fear chose to make weapons, numbing drugs and to radiate our food.

Why were we so afraid? We seemed so angry and lonely. I feel shame for what we have become but I feel compassion for our suffering. We were in such an internal turmoil that we did all we could to survive with the awareness we had. We were simply deafened and blinded by fear.

All was laying in front of our eyes ready to be put together, all the pieces of the puzzle at our reach to embrace the wisdom of our ancestors, their forgotten voices and our modern voices of science and technology. We had all the necessary elements to embrace the wisdom that would set us free, just as it was spoken in the story of creation of 'Tule':

> *All is interconnected, we are all one.*
> *Death is simply a bridge between worlds.*

All is consciousness breathing...

We had all that was needed to merge Spirituality and Science, creating a new map of the human psyche and of reality that would allow us to evolve even further and create harmonic ripples instead of turmoil and violence.

The effects of the spinning wheel of greed were too strong. Once we human beings lived in fear it was impossible for us to listen. We chose not to listen. We didn't listen to ourselves, to our ancestors or to the voices of our own scientific evolution. We choose to remain attached to primitive ideas of a material linear world created by a 'god' separate from us. How could we? How could we not see the obvious? It saddens my heart and I feel guilty for having been part of such a display of ignorance...

Entry: Lucia:
Start call back. Subject in emotional distress. Frequency down o.8hz.

Wait!! Wait! If reality is not really linear, if the atom is not solid but also waves of energy vibrating, if the observer affects the result of the experiment and if these waves are outside time and space...then, then this is not a set outcome, this is more like a dream! A dream of the future that is not solid, it is a possibility, a wave of possibility, but not a definite outcome.

If the outcome depends on the observer, what would happen if I go back and dream a different dream, a dream where we break free from the shackles of fear and where we listen?...
Lucia, wait! I can hear the voice of 'Tule' whispering through the wind:

"If what appears as perceived does not exist, whatever appears as perceiver does not exist; Due to this, there is also a rationale behind the breakthrough to freedom from this appearance of perceived and perceiver, because without beginning a volatile state prevails; and duality's not existing at all is what really exists."

Your ancestor Maitreya left this treaty many cycles before you were born so you could remember to choose wisely your dream. Dream, dreamer! Dream!"

*"The lips of wisdom are closed, except
to the ears of Understanding.
1.The ALL IS MIND; the Universe is
'mental'.
2.As Above, so below; as below so
above.
3.Nothing rests; everything moves;
everything vibrates.
4.Everything is Dual; everything has
poles; everything has its pair of
opposites.
5.Everything flows, out and in;
everything has its tides; all things rise
and fall.
6.Every Cause has its Effect; every
Effect has its Cause.
7.Gender is in everything; everything
has its Masculine and Feminine
Principles; Gender manifests in all
planes."*
(The Kybalion)

Section Three
Leap of Faith

"Leap because you want to, not because you have to. But if you find yourself in the free fall, stop falling and start flying"
Ná Áak

Chapter X
Choice

The Leap of Faith that I see as necessary for human survival is:

> Let go of the need to rationalise the Universe
> and rather immerse ourselves in the *experience* of the Universe.

The choice to dream is not a matter of knowledge but a matter of
HEART

Can I Love and accept myself enough to care about the dream that I
am immersed in?   Can I Love and accept myself enough to
experience that I am not only separate but 'ONE' with all of creation
at the same time?   Can I Love and accept myself enough to do
something about it?

Our future is yet to be created and not to be forecasted, as Ervin
Laszlo, one of the strong voices leading today's world quantum shift,
would suggest. We have individual and collective responsibility for
the reality that appears in front of our eyes. According to what we
know today from quantum mechanics the universe is something
similar to a big ocean of waves that materialise when the observer
dreams a dream for it. The information from our conscious and
unconscious gives shape to this vast ocean and makes it appear real
and solid.

The big dream we are living is both an individual dream and a
collective dream at the same time. We are unity and community,
and both aspects of reality cannot be separated from one another.
One exists because of the existence of the other and vice-versa. This
paradox is what we explore in the myth of creation when
consciousness becomes dual but at the same time it remains whole.
This is the sacred trinity of Ometeotl as the one ocean of
consciousness undifferentiated, undefined and infinite, and the two-
feathered dragons Ometecutli and Omecihuatl representing the
sacred couple, the experience of duality and separation.

According to this understanding, we are the ones dreaming the world into being; we are 'The One' who is dreaming.

This same wisdom is what we hear from mysticism and indigenous wisdom from around the world: the universe in an interconnected web of consciousness as the absolute reality that permeates all that exists; and the reality of phenomena or apparent separation, the reality of observer and observed as the relative reality, the illusion that appears to our senses as we are incarnated in a human body.

The mystics and medicine people who lived from this understanding remained in harmony with the Earth and the Universe, always seeing beyond the illusion of phenomena into the interconnectedness of all creation. When a mystic sees a mountain it sees itself experiencing the world as a mountain and therefore the mountain is sacred to him/her because it is the same consciousness that makes it possible for him/her to be alive and breathing.

In the same manner when the mystics see another human being, they only see themselves having a different experience of life, they do not see 'THING's' , they see 'Thou' their brothers and sisters. From this perspective, life becomes immediately sacred to the mystic because all that happens in any part of creation is as if it is happening to him/her. All is simply an extension of the one sacred body of the divine creative consciousness. When living from this place, respect for life and creation becomes common sense and not something that has to be taught in school. Respecting life becomes a natural action and it is not a quality to be attained but an intrinsic part of one's being.

In the moment we cut or trim the sacred trinity and decide to forget or deny any of its aspects, we lose sacred balance and our dreams are no longer dreams of RAINBOW light that allow all to coexist. Instead we become fractured spectrums of light, not knowing where we came from or where we are going. In that moment, as a fractured spectrum of light, we then believe that the fractured life is all there is as the only real and true reality; we become ignorant to the interconnectedness of life and the universe and we allow separation to rule our existence.

When separate, we fail to see the sacredness of life, creation and, of course, of other human beings. That is when we all walk as fractured spectrums of light not caring for anything other than our own fractured existence. We become <u>ITS</u> and so does the whole of creation. All are simply fractured pieces of rock, wood, meat and metal to exploit to our individual convenience and will.

A fractured spectrum of light fails to see the connection with the beam of light that creates it and in the ignorance of our fractured state we become afraid and crave for that connection that we know within ourselves but fail to find inside. We then try to find purpose, meaning and wholeness outside of ourselves by attaching to other fractured spectrums of light. Possessions become important; money or people giving us a fractured sense of who and what we are. What people think of us becomes important because it gives us a sense of who we are. The letters that follow our name become important because that gives us the illusion of power. Having children becomes important because it provides a sense of purpose; finding validation in different communities and religions gives shape to our personality and beliefs, and so on.

All of these aspects of life are certainly relevant and part of life experience but they are only tiny aspects of the bigger picture of creation. The illusion lies in believing that this is all we have to provide us with purpose and meaning.

When we find ourselves stuck in that place then life becomes a quest to posses the people, titles and fame that will give us purpose; it becomes a quest to walk everybody else's path except our own. We become followers and lose our sovereignty in trying to fit into the boxes that someone else has drawn, oblivious to the fact that to fit ourselves into the boxes we have to trim and cut ourselves down in order to be acceptable to others, losing our precious uniqueness and individuality.

If we read the book of nature, as mystics and medicine people did and still do, we realise that our eyes can distinguish trees from the rest of creation, and among these trees we can distinguish many hundreds of types of trees, all presenting different common aspects.

If we are to select one, for example Tule, we know that it is a *Taxodium mucronatum (Cypress or Ahuehuete)* and we can distinguish clearly its differences from an Oak or a Beech Tree. In spite of that we cannot find two Tule's that are identical. Each one is harmonious and beautiful in its own right and blends perfectly with its environment. But somehow our human thinking has led us to make a design of the perfect Tule and then a mould or box in which all Tule trees must fit. As a result, we cannot tell one Tule from another and we end up in a GREY world.

I remember when my western education wanted to get me to think like my teachers. But I had been shaped so well with indigenous wisdom that no matter how well I could understand Freud or Rogers, I could never fit in the box they had made for me because my branches of indigenous wisdom and natural medicine practice were outside of the permitted boundaries of the box, actually scratching the boxes of abnormal and maladaptive behaviour. I was asked to give up my 'COLOURNESS' to fit into the 'GREY' box. I have witnessed thousands of examples like this around the globe. People feeling depressed and with no purpose because they have been forced into so many narrow boxes that there is hardly anything left of who they truly are.

Tule as a fractured spectrum.   *Tule dissected into boxes.*

Just as there are types of trees, there are patterns to follow, archetypes and ratios that repeat in the continuous unfolding universe. This is what I refer to as: the COLOURNESS of each individual. To find your COLOURNESS is to reconnect with who you are, with your ancestors, with your lineage, with your archetype, your voice, your sound, your dance; it is finding your tribe. It does not mean to fit in a box but to find the spectrum of light that resonates more with your true self, it is the exercise of finding **more** about who you are, not less; it is to expand your perspective of self from the conditioned boxes of who you think you are to the transpersonal picture of who you truly are; it means expanding into the whole of your being and stop trying to fit into pre-defined boxes.

Finding COLOURNESS does not necessarily form a RAINBOW, we still have to be willing to give up our individual existence to access a collective experience as the RAINBOW. Only when we are willing to detach from the over-identification with COLOUR can we create the masterpiece of the RAINBOW symphony, where every instrument can play their tune and at the same time follow a common map of sound and silence, where we are all collaborating together as one, in the same way that Tule lives harmoniously with its Tule brothers and sisters and with the Earth.

In that moment the miracle of a masterpiece is made, and just as in nature, no sound ever becomes too loud but all flows in perfect harmony. So can we, as sovereign individuals, play together without silencing anyone or giving more importance to anyone, simply allowing the difference of every colour to manifest and be part of the whole.

When we can attune ourselves to the collective dream and play the RAINBOW symphony then we will see that the RAINBOW only exists out of one single beam of light, the one origin to all the COLOURS, the one origin to us all and to all of creation, THE ONE consciousness. In this manner we do not find not power and control for the symphony to be performed but organic hierarchy, which requires every individual to be responsible for their own performance. The Light conducts the orchestra but does not dominate it. It lets it be, if one instrument -or colour-plays out of tune, transforms the music piece into disharmonious noise. This is community living in equality and organic order, every piece vital and equal in importance for the symphony to happen.

What incapacitates us to move from GREYNESS and a fractured existence into COLOURNESS; from COLOURNESS into RAINBOWNESS; from RAINBOWNESS into LIGHT, and from LIGHT into EMPTINESS, are our well known friends:

Fear, Anger, Desire, Depression, Jealousy and Greed.

The Leap of Faith that we can choose to take is to first accept that we are 'Ignorant'. When I am able to confidently say 'I AM IGNORANT' then I can do something about it.

If we are not willing to take this first Leap of Faith our future is easy to forecast, an outcome no different to what we see around us, only bigger and louder.

If a person is having a nightmare but knows it is only a nightmare and that he or she can wake up, then the nightmare is no more. But when the person is having a nightmare and does not know she is asleep, the nightmare will keep on playing eternally. This is hell. We become trapped in hell, not out of punishment for being a sinner; but because we are ignorant to the fact that we are dreaming a nightmare. As soon as the person realises: Ah! This is only a dream!, then the person can wake up from the hellish nightmare and CHOOSE another dream.

When we refuse to accept we are dreaming, we become puppets of our dream. We are victims of our own ignorance. We lose sovereignty as we become like a feather in a stormy sea, with no direction and no possibility of steering our journey. This glittery and violent puppet show ends only with us waking up and finding our own capacity to:

CHOOSE the DREAM

Many have woken up to this realisation and have worked hard in choosing new dreams and manifesting different dreams, but have failed to address all the aspects of the self that make possible the dreaming in the first place. They very rapidly take to the idea of dreaming differently but they do not like to admit that if they were dreaming a nightmare it was because they suffered from ignorance in the first place, and dreaming a new dream from inside the nightmare only brings a more disastrous outcome. Because what we are doing is superimposing a new image onto the nightmare and this is called denial. Denial can be worse than not knowing we are asleep because this person believes they have woken up when in fact they haven't. They fail to comprehend the complexity and subtle layers of reality and believe they have arrived, wherever that is, denying their human ignorance and unconsciousness.

The challenge then remains: Can I accept 'I AM IGNORANT'. No matter how many masters and degrees precede my name, and how many self-help books I have read, or how many years I have been meditating, or how many courses I have taken?

Remember that no matter where you see yourself to be in the evolutionary scale, when you deny your natural human limitations, you truncate your evolution, because you are taking as the absolute reality the state of being that you are currently living and experiencing.

You stop your growth because you believe you know it all and you have processed it all, while you are still trapped in IRON reality. No matter what language you use in your life, whether your work is buying and selling, teaching, doing surgery, psychoanalysing, empowering people, motivating, coaching, healing, if you believe you are no longer ignorant you have truncated your evolution and you believe then that all there is to the universe is what you know already. You are still dissecting Tule in boxes, failing to comprehend the limitless infinite and eternal characteristic of creation.

Ignorance opens the doors for expanding, unfolding, creating, dreaming, evolving. Accepting Ignorance is accepting growth and manifestation, it is to permanently welcome that there is an unknown universe yet to be woken up to.

Once I have accepted my Ignorance the next Leap of Faith is to understand the reasons why I am ignorant, by understanding the patterns, programs, conditioning and experiences individually and collectively, that informed and created my personal nightmare or experience of life. It is the step where I learn and explore all the possible experiences that imprinted the code of my being. It is when I learn about what makes me who I am and understand what a human being is and what human experience means.

This step implies the commitment to stop generating more 'karma', meaning to stop reacting unconsciously in action, speech and thought. When we swim in the ocean of consciousness, every single movement, speech and thought creates a ripple effect that cannot be cancelled. The ripples will spread through the ocean returning to us the same ripples that we generated; just like a mirror image - whatever we send out gets reflected back to us. Before you can save a man that is drowning you have to get him to calm down. If not, you will drown and sink with him. In the same manner, if we are trying to rescue ourselves from drowning but we are in panic creating turmoil in the water then there is very little we can do.

First generate no more ripples. Become still and conscious of action, speech and thought. When you remain still then you can look at the place where you are and observe your surroundings so you can do something about it. Then you can consciously choose your actions.

> Action before stillness only draws the same action,
> but amplified a thousand-fold.

It is then that the third Leap of Faith has to be taken by engaging in a conscious path of inner contemplation where I can find myself and where I can not only realise I am asleep, but I experience that I am asleep so I can gently wake up from that state. This is when we can discern which patterns are not serving us well by detaching from the physical, emotional and intellectual illusions, by detaching from the material possessions, emotional reactions and thought patterns that create the nightmare of suffering. Detaching does not imply 'not to care' but rather to understand the illusory essence of the world of phenomena. This is when we resolve our karmic patterns, when we cut ties with the old and evolve.

The last and most important step becomes, then, the path to follow in order to code new experiences, in order to input new algorithms in the computer of your being so it can start dreaming a different dream. This is when, after stillness, and no more unconscious ripples created, you choose carefully which ripples to generate. This aspect can be the most difficult because it requires resilience, commitment and self-discipline. The old patterns will fight hard not to die and, just like entities in their own right, they are attached to you find it hard to let go and that is when relapse happens. These patterns will not die when you make them conscious and become aware of them, they will die when you stop feeding them. To know about the pattern helps us greatly to gain self-awareness but does not necessarily stop the pattern from emerging or playing itself out.

We can also experience the pattern in an expanded state of awareness trough trance-induced experiences, but again although the experience will bring you a deeper realisation than the knowing, it will not necessarily stop the pattern. Only the everyday discipline and resilience of not feeding the pattern will have permanent effects in your being. We recognise and know the pattern, we make friends with it; we experience it by becoming it and understanding its ripple effects; but then we consciously engage in a life of practicing the discipline that helps us best to remain still and stop feeding the pattern.

There is a vital key to this process to be successful and that is:

IGNORANCE

It is not a typo I meant IGNORANCE Because we tend to expect that as far as we have followed this cycle once or, as some more generous people would think, twice or ten times, the pattern will cease and be over and then we are no longer ignorant, only to realise that we have again truncated our development.

When Ignorance becomes your dear friend you understand that the layers of existence are infinite and subtle and individual as well as collective, so the patterns will keep replaying like a film as far as you embody the human apparatus that makes the experience possible. Today in Transpersonal psychology this is called COEX (*system of condensed experiences, S.Grof*). As the wheel of life spins through the spiral of evolution, the patterns replay in search for resolution or meaning. This causes many people to feel disillusioned in life about their spiritual practice because they see after a few years that the old circumstances recreate themselves over and over. When an experience repeats itself in life, it is simply a manifestation of the natural cycle of the unfolding universe as it seeks experience, and every time it presents itself in your dream you have a new opportunity to choose how to complete, resolve, react or deny it.

It is also relevant to say that when in sleep state, being a puppet of the nightmare, the nightmare repeats itself like a broken record because it is the only record playing in your nightmare.

These experiences are accumulated in the holographic universe in the collective consciousness that dates from the beginning of time and lasts until the end of time. The universe is eternal, so experience is always playing in one form or another and what changes when we take Leaps of Faith is the capacity to choose which experiences and dreams you decide to engage with instead of being a puppet of 'karma' (past, present and future individual and collective actions). In effect, you change your place in the game of life from being 'played out' to being a player.

As we slowly and continuously regain our sovereignty and capacity to choose and be responsible for our dream, we move towards 'enlightenment.' As we learn from the teachers of Death (letting go) and Ignorance, we detach from the illusions of the world of phenomena and live more and more grounded and sitting in the lotus of the reality of unity or pure being. The illusions of the world of phenomena can come in physical or material form, in emotional form as emotions or in intellectual form as thoughts. Detachment from the illusion in all its forms is necessary when striving towards realisation.

I remember once in a session with a realised master from India, a woman was asking the Guru why she had to have a practice when all the books she was reading were telling her that she was divine consciousness and therefore 'whole' just as she was. She felt that if the theory behind the practice that we are all Light was true then that meant that she was already realised and there was no need to follow a method towards enlightenment. The Guru smiled graciously to the translation of the question and proceeded to tell a story. He said that once in India there was a man who seemed to have attained realisation while meditating, so the Guru put a hot coal on his leg to confirm if this was true. The hot coal rested on his leg and the man did not react. He remains in the realised state he had attained. After some time he came back to the present because of a burning smell. In that moment the Guru knew this person had attained realisation. The Guru then said to the woman: "I cannot say to you that you are not realised. If you believe you are realised then you are. If so, maybe we can try a burning coal on your leg so you can confirm you are."

Our ego-mind, although necessary for a human experience, can be our worst enemy when in a sleep state.

> Leap and Choose your dream by realising:
> I am ignorant,
> Understanding why I am ignorant,
> Waking up from ignorance,
> Remaining awake.

If science confirms what indigenous wisdom and mysticism have been saying for centuries, then this means that the only one responsible for the dream or the nightmare is:

YOU

You are the one who is 'The One'.

Nobody is stuck in suffering against their will. We are stuck because we are unaware we are asleep. To cease suffering we need to:

WAKEN IN
To awake to the inner self, to open the inner eye..

What is the legacy that you wish to leave behind for your children? Do you wish them to swim into turbulent waters difficult to navigate because so many unconscious ripples make it impossible for the ocean to flow in a harmonious pattern? Or do you wish them to swim in still waters that can be navigated and that allow natural and strong waves to emerge so people can surf on them?

Suffering and violence creates turbulent waters. Compassion and love creates still waters with currents that are harmonious and strong. It is up to you to choose. Are you willing to Leap?

"If an engagement is sure

To bring victory,
And yet the ruler
Forbids it,
Fight;
If an engagement is sure
To bring defeat,
And yet the ruler
Orders it,
Do not fight.
He who advances
Without seeking
Fame,
Who retreats
Without escaping
Blame,
He whose one aim is
To protect his people
And serve his Lord,
This man is
A Jewel of the Realm."
(Sun Tzu, The Art of War)

Section Four
Awakening Consciousness

"The return of 'Quetzalcoatl' is not 'out there', it is 'in there', in you. You are the Awakened Consciousness; you are who is dreaming the Dream, you are who is living the Dream"
Ná Áak

Section Four
Awakening Consciousness

Chapter XI
Actualisation of Self

Who am I?
Who am I? Who am I? Who am I?
Who am I? Who am I? Who am I?
Who am I? Who am I? Who am I? Who am I? Who am I? Who am I? ....

The conceptualisation of 'who I am' is defined by your conscious awareness and belief of what defines you as a human being. In order to actualise and update the understanding of who you are, you need to make it your business to know and experience your humanness. We have allowed the practices of religion, science, psychiatry, philosophy and psychology to study the human body and mind and give us the answer to the question: 'Who am I? These practices define the boxes that we make ourselves fit into.

All practices provide a vital key and piece to the puzzle of the Universe. Every part that unfolds is relevant to the mystery of humanness; if we decide to eliminate parts or pieces of the puzzle, we will be left with an incomplete picture of reality. Some pieces naturally will oppose themselves because duality is a natural part of the material experience. To put together the puzzle it does not mean that all the pieces have to be the same colour and shape. That is no puzzle. A puzzle has infinite shapes and colours and some pieces will contradict one another, forming in that contradiction the union. A complete puzzle is one that includes all pieces and accepts difference as an essential aspect of creation. There is no right and wrong, there is only uniqueness and patterns that repeat and show themselves throughout the evolution of uniqueness.

Taking into consideration the maps from ancestral lineages of Indigenous Wisdom and Mysticism, and the present maps from our rational and technological evolution from Psychology and Quantum Science, we can define the experience of the Universe and creation as:

Phenomena and Pure Being

Our human experience is a mirror-like projection of Phenomena that unfolds from Pure Being outwards and inwards, following sacred geometry ratios, only to contract inwards and outwards as it returns to source. Pure Being remaining the source, absolute, still and ultimately empty in nature. Ometeotl, the unified field (Higgs boson), and Phenomena the experience of duality. Ometecutli and Omecihuatl (matter – antimatter, ying – yang) expanding and contracting.

Between the outward and inward dual expansion and unravelling of Phenomena, in the middle lies the lotus throne of Pure Being as the observer, as 'The One' extra particle that makes creation possible. The Universe balancing itself in the dance of Unity, 'The One' Pure Being and its Phenomena and separation into a dual and paired manifestation. This point of consciousness observes the dance of Phenomena as infinite possible reflections of the Pure Being, remaining still and detached from all experiences observed, permeating it all and creating it all.

The intentions of expansion and contraction are the out-breath and in-breath of Pure Being. In India this flow of Pure Being is called Prāna, in China Chi, in different shamanic traditions Spirit, in ancient Greece Pneuma, in Tibet Tsog-lung.

Expanding from Pure Being unravels the web of consciousness. This web in its subtle and non-material aspects we will refer as 'MIND' and in its material and gross aspects we will refer as 'BODY'. These 'MIND' and 'BODY' aspects of creation expand hand-in-hand with its mirror image of what we could call 'anti-MIND' and 'anti-BODY' or, to add drama, we can say: 'demonic-MIND' and demonic-BODY' vs 'angelic-MIND' and 'angelic-BODY'.

These subtle and gross aspects of creation emerge from the source, from the one consciousness, never separating from it but simply elongating, just like a rubber band.

In both we can find elements that are part of the individual experience of the manifested Phenomena (being) and elements that belong to the collective experience common to all of creation.

There are infinite subtle and gross layers of Phenomena manifestations that expand in a circular array north - south, east - west and above – below, for both mirror images of 'MIND' and 'anti-MIND'. These directions serve as vectors or pointers that grid the bardos or realms of Phenomena, providing a map of coordinates that can be interpreted according to the values of its vibratory frequency, its manifested shape and its parallel alternative. All happening in our experience as past and future are only an illusion that can be differentiated when the vibratory frequency has slowed down enough to perceive temporality in slow motion but not to the extent that no motion can be perceived.

Interconnection and Correspondence

Although, for the purpose of explaining the human experience, we are differentiating the parts from the 'whole', these parts do not exist independently of one another. They co-exist and are interconnected and interdependent. Just as a reflection in the mirror cannot exist without the object that is being reflected in the first place, the 'anti-MIND' cannot be reflected without the 'MIND'. In the same manner this concept applies to all forms that emerge from Pure Being so the 'BODY' cannot manifest its reflection without the 'MIND' that creates the reflection.

The 'BODY' cannot simply manifest as a fractured spectrum of light or an isolated event. This mirror-like nature of the universe doesn't cease to exist because we fail to consciously comprehend and experience it. This is part of Quantum Mechanics in the subtle expressions, and Quantum Physiology in the gross expressions; all is interconnected, and each part is a thread in the pattern weaved by creation.

If Phenomena were to separate itself from Pure Being, the outcome would be instant extermination, as both pairs of opposites of Dual Phenomenology would cancel each other out. What makes the dance of Duality possible is the existence of Pure Being as 'The One' field of consciousness that permeates all. In the same manner, Pure being experiences itself through the experience of its opposite, Phenomena and Duality. The sacred trinity, Unity and Duality, dancing at the core of creation.

When we apply this to the human experience we find a comprehensive general map of the human experience that holds and contains it. This map is not a definite territory but simply a reference point to evolve together with our awakening. This map shows the basic template, from which its more complex detail unravels:

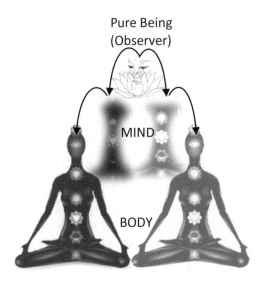

The next template that we will examine for the purpose of the actualisation of Self is the three-fold nature of the subtle and gross manifestations of the 'MIND' and 'BODY':

Physical
Causal (Intellectual)
Astral (Emotional)

The physical, causal and astral 'MIND' and 'BODY' are layers that contain the collective and individual information about the phenomenological manifestation of what is being born. These layers will, in equal manner, record new experiences in the form of physical, causal and astral energies as the human experience is taking place. The experience will be experienced at all times both externally and internally, as the unfolding is always outwards and inwards. The external senses that will record the experience are the physical senses such as vision, hearing, smell, taste and touch and internally the inner eye will constantly record the inward universe.

Each layer will act both as part and whole, interconnected and interdependent on one another. Physicality, causality and astrality will always inform each other and be directly connected. Separation of physical symptoms, causal or intellectual symptoms and astral or emotional symptoms without considering the others will give an incomplete and incorrect diagnosis.

The next stop is the differentiation of the three main channels or strings of Tsog-lung (Prāna):

- Uma or central channel (Sushumnā)
- Roma or solar channel (Pingalā)
- Rkyan ma or lunar channel (īdā)

These channels of energy can be observed in the archetypal realms, just as we spoke about Ometeotl, Ometecutli and Omecihuatl, as if looking at them with telescopic vision, again both inwards as non-material forms (deities) and outwards as material forms (planets and galaxies). We can also observe them at a microscopic level as manifested inwards (waves or fields) and outwards (DNA, atoms, particles). This is best understood in experience rather than rationalisation, because very rapidly you can deduce that the inward reality overlaps with the outward reality, and the microscopic vision overlaps with the telescopic vision. This is because of the principle of Interconnection and the mirror-like nature of the Pure Being manifested into Phenomena. All is an unfolding Spiral that, if followed, will always take you to the one same starting point or source, Pure Being.

Moving forward in the map of manifestation, the next natural step is to look over at the main focal points of intersection of the tsog-lung channels. The place where the 'Roma' (Pingalā) and the 'Rkyan ma' (īdā) intersect with the Uma (Sushumnā) is called Chakra. These energy centres facilitate the flow of Tsog-lung or Prāna throughout the 'BODY' and 'MIND'.

Sahasrāra Cakra	Crown Chakra
Ājñā Cakra	Wisdom-eye Chakra
Visuddha Cakra	Throat Chakra
Anāhata Cakra	Heart Chakra
Manipura Cakra	Solar Plexus Chakra
Svāadhishthāna Cakra	Creative Chakra
Mūlādhāra Cakra	Base Chakra

These Chakras correspond to the different elements that make life possible. The elements interact with each other in a symbiotic manner. All of these energy channels and symbiosis of elements is described in detail in the books of medicine of traditions that emerged from China, India and Tibet among others. It is described in such detail that up to 72,000 branches of these mystical nerves can be differentiated and treated accordingly.

It is not for this chapter to enter into that detail but certainly we can observe how different traditions created maps that can easily be superimposed and that contain the same essential elements of creation. Each map follows its mythology and culture according to the themes that were part of the environment of the different tribes.

What it is relevant to mention is that each element is associated with the physical manifestation of the human biology and physiology, where every organ is observed as an individual manifestation and as a part of the whole body.

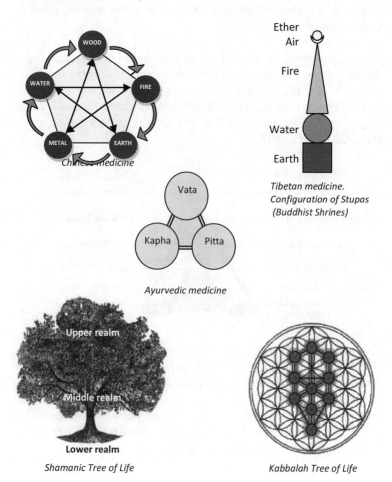

Chinese medicine

Ether
Air

Fire

Water

Earth

Tibetan medicine.
Configuration of Stupas
(Buddhist Shrines)

Ayurvedic medicine

Shamanic Tree of Life

Kabbalah Tree of Life

<u>Conscious, Unconscious and Subconscious aspects of the Ego Self.</u>

Pure Being (the observer) is the anchor point of both inner and outer experiences while creation unfolds in non-material and subtle form and in material and gross form, in 'MIND' and 'BODY', slowly forming the Ego Self. All that is known to the Ego Self is its conscious experience. All that is unknown to its 'BODY' and 'MIND' remains unconscious and although real and playing in the background, the being fails to notice its presence and is unaware of it.

The in-between place from consciousness to unconsciousness is the sub-conscious aspect, where as the Self wakens up it can access this buffer of information which is processed and ready to be integrated by it. The Ego Self can jump into the vastness of the ocean that is unconscious to it, but it can only bring fully into consciousness what it can comprehend physically, intellectually and emotionally. The rest, although experienced and seen, remains in the sub-conscious until it can be fully integrated, and only then it can it become part of the conscious experience, as conscious equals self-awareness.

From this perspective, the concept of conscious and unconscious are not aspects of the psyche of the human experience but they refer more to the state of awakening in which the individual finds itself immerse into. They relate to ignorance as far as what we are conscious of we are not ignorant to, and what we are unconscious of we are ignorant to. Seeing the Unconscious does not make us stop being ignorant. Only the conscious and constant discipline of an awakened life makes the integration of the unconscious possible, waking us up from ignorance into enlightenment.

We could say that the more conscious we become, the closer we are to realisation and the less effort the Ego Self has to make to remain awake. The more unconscious we are, the more effort we have to make to remain awake.

Ego Self

This aspect of humanness is the one that tells me 'I am' and gives the scope of vision to the Observer or Pure Being. The Pure Being is awake to all and conscious to all because it is the source of the infinite and eternal universe that was, that is and that will be. We cannot say that the Pure Being suddenly becomes unconscious or ignorant when it incarnates in human form. On the contrary, it remains permanently awake and in what is known as enlightened state.

When we incarnate into human form, as co-creators, Pure Being is dressed with a collective and individual 'MIND' and 'BODY' which manifests in the physical realm, in the causal (intellectual) realm and in the astral (emotional) realm. It is this dress that composes the Ego Self. As the Pure Being is dressed with the collective and individual karma and Akashic memory, crystal clear awareness starts becoming blurred, as if the mirror image suddenly becomes distorted or smoked, narrowing the scope of vision according to the information recorded in the layers that we acquire.

The layers of the 'MIND' and 'BODY' that make us who we are a recollection of previous occurrences, experiences and karma (action). If we have created many ripples in the ocean every time we have incarnated, then the coats will be big and thick. It is as if the more waves we have created the less we are free to steer our being into a specific incarnation, so what occurs is that we get drawn into the body we incarnate as a result of the turmoil we left in the waters before.

It is important to clarify that karma and its effects are more complex than a linear understanding of past lives and reincarnations. Remember that the layers are vast and all reality is interconnected in a single web of information. So when we go back into the ocean of Pure Being, when we die, some of us raises back from that ocean mixed with thousands of other parts and experiences. It is like a big pot of chunky soup where every incarnation is a scoop from the pot with chunky bits: I eat some of it and the rest goes back to the pot where it mixes again with the whole soup. Then I take another scoop with a few chunky bits that got stuck from the previous scoop and many other bits that are new. Although certain elements of karma can be traced it is not a linear and causal science and it always involves collective and individual information that transcends rational understanding.

The Ego Self is necessary to experience humanness as it filters the information of the Pure Being through physical sensations, intellectual thoughts and emotions. The Ego Self makes it possible to experience life and walk the path of unravelling all the coats that blind our vision in order to attain realisation. It provides the Pure Being with the equipment to have an experience of itself. Without Ego Self, or if it's fractured, split or weak, the flow of information from the Universe becomes overwhelming to the individual and functioning in a human body becomes almost impossible.

When the Ego Self is able to expand its scope it can experience 'mystical insight' as it opens its vision into the reality of Pure Being. This can happen spontaneously or it can be induced by bringing the 'MIND' and 'BODY' into a trance-like state. Today we know of many paths to induce Pure Being experiences and insight such as the traditional rites of passage in indigenous cultures using ritual dance, singing, piercing, tattoo, extremes of temperature or ascetic practices such as silence, fasting, prayer, meditation and breathing. Some of these rituals and practices include the use of psychotropic plants.

When these experiences happen spontaneously and the person is not equipped to understand or filter the experience, instead of a state of 'mystical insight or realisation what appears is a state of disorder and chaos driving the person into spiritual emergency. Today these states are understood by biological psychiatry under the labels of psychosis, delusions, hallucinations and maladaptive behaviour, but the evolution of transpersonal psychiatry and psychology has opened room for these experiences to find meaning, completion and help the person to regain functionality as they are a natural part of being alive.

The Ego Self can be strengthened to serve as the filter of a human experience, containing and holding it, and not as a blinding obstacle and enemy of the experience. When the Ego Self experiences detachment of its 'I AM-ness' it can have a similar role as the observer when in human form: still, awake and in contemplation and awe of life.

Memory

Both the Pure Being and the Phenomena have a memory. Memories of experiences are retained just like algorithms in all the infinite layers of the 'MIND' and 'BODY'. Memory is not restricted to a conscious recollection of individual ideas and concepts, but is the holographic encoded image and patterns of all experiences ever experienced and of all experiences yet to be experienced individually and collectively. It is what is commonly called 'Akashic Records' or 'Akashic Field'. This field unfolds and expands together with creation as it is contained in the essence of the Pure Being. It is the code or layout that consciousness follows as it enters a dual experience. From this perspective we can say that holographic information permeates it all as the binary code behind Phenomena.

Imagination

Between the reality unfolding inwards and the reality unfolding outwards remains a bridge of communication commonly called Imagination. This is not an aspect of the psyche that provides fantasy, delusions or hallucinations, but rather remains as the connecting telescopic and microscopic eye to the outer and inner realities. It is the inner sense of the Ego Self.

Individuation and Impermanence

The entrance and the exit from Pure Being into the world of Phenomena and vice-versa happens through Death. Death acts as the world bridge, as the passage from one reality into another, as the connection between out-breath and in-breath, giving the world of Phenomena its impermanent nature. This constant movement and change is what allows Phenomena to evolve and acquire complexity of being. Every time the bridge of Death has to be crossed the Akashic field records the experience and then it plays the algorithm of the experience throughout the journey of the manifested form.

There are many sacred scriptures that describe in detail the different realms or bardos of existence that we cross when entering and leaving the body. Thanks to the perseverance of minds like Stan Grof, today we have clear maps of the macroscopic and microscopic implications of these experiences.

The term Individuation, although introduced by Carl G. Jung in psychology, refers to the natural spiral of evolution that Death is a catalyst for, the natural evolution towards wholeness, unity, the way back home to Pure Being from the existence of Phenomena. This natural intrinsic force of life is constantly stretching the capacity and complexity of the Ego Self or being. As we explored before, the Universe is following a constant movement of expansion and contraction, of out-breath and in-breath, life, death and rebirth. This natural rhythm makes the Universe impermanent and in constant flow. This cyclical waltz has a pattern of order and chaos, expansion and contraction, manifestation and dissolution. We can see this pattern repeating itself throughout all forms of life facilitating the polishing of the Ego Self, waking up to our true self. This eternal cosmic breath takes us through the journey of individuation or enlightenment.

The spiral and eternal rhythm of individuation can be summarised as:

1) **Output Order** Water. Known and established order. Union.

2) **Input Chaos** Earth. Change in established order. Dissolution.

3) **Output Chaos** Fire. Response to the Chaos. Separation.

4) **Input Order** Air. New order established. Differentiation.

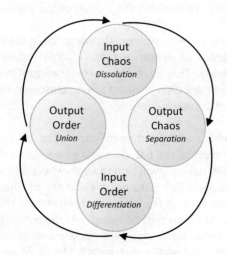

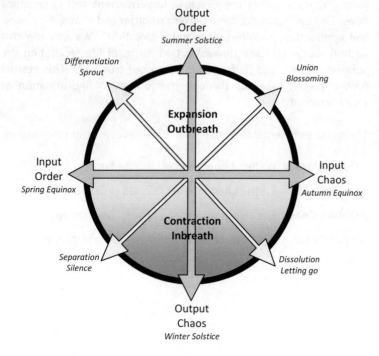

> *"As we rest in the known order, in unity, time to blossom, death comes to visit marking the end of the order, dissolving it into chaos, time to let go; as we find ourselves in chaos we are separated out, time for silence; we move out of chaos into a new differentiation, time to sprout. This will become our known order and union, in there we bloom, only to wait for the next wave of chaos to come in."* Ná Áak

This natural cycle can be observed in all manifested Phenomena and is the basic template of macrocosmic and microcosmic cycles. In the moment we incarnate into human form the finger print of our life gets imprinted or encoded in our 'MIND' and 'BODY', giving us readings through the physical body, our thought patterns and our emotional states and reactions. This is the relevance of observing and consciously engaging in how we enter into the world and how we exit.

Temporality

This aspect of reality does not imply time as understood in western thinking but cyclical movement. All ancient calendars are based on the cosmic rhythm of individuation. Temporality is an experience of the conscious self when it has incarnated to a point where the vibratory frequency has slowed down enough to experience it in slow motion and still preserve enough speed to appear in motion.

The branches and implications of the templates we reviewed are infinite and they can be either simple and direct like in-breath and out-breath, or extremely complex and intricate like particles and antiparticles, boson, leptons, etc.

The existence of Pure Being and Phenomena are regulated by a few core principles:

Pure Being is all there is. It is empty in nature.

Phenomena unfolds as it vibrates into dual pairs of opposites as a reflection of Pure Being, following the rhythm of cosmic breath and individuation. All experiences of Phenomena are imprinted in the Akashic field of Pure Being, creating input and output ripples.

*"...man cannot stand meaningless life,
we need more understanding of human nature
because the only real danger that exists is man
himself.
He is the great danger and we are pitifully
unaware of it. We know nothing of man, far too
little.
Its psyche should be studied because we are the
origin of all coming evil"
(1959 interview Carl Gustav Jung)*

Chapter XII
Applying the Actualisation

'AHIMSA' non-violence

अहिंसा

The actualisation of self takes place as we become the actualisation itself, not when we memorise, rationalise or conceptualise it. This can only happen in the Heart, in union with the realisation that Pure Being is the supreme source or quantum field of all creation; it can only happen by conscious experience.

We don't accidentally fall into realisation; we have to walk our way into it. Insight and understanding can happen spontaneously, but only the conscious state of integrating the new insight in experiential form - physically, intellectually and emotionally - will transform the Self. In Friedrich Nietzsche words: "He who would learn to fly one day must first learn to stand and walk and run and climb and dance; one cannot fly into flying"

To practice non-violence does not mean to practice non-action but rather acceptance, acceptance of what is. When we fight and struggle against the natural flow of creation we live out of violent speech, thought and action. When we deny pain, illness, aging and death we are being violent to the Self because we are trying to make out of life something that it is not. We have used our scientific and technological evolution to try to create a world that is permanent and never changing, where the birth of our children is artificial and scheduled; where the real colour of the hair is disguised; where the skin is pulled, poisoned and cut to erase its natural aging; where illness and pain are numbed and covered up with plasters so we don't have to look at its real causes; and where the dying are abandoned in hospitals and homes only to be left to die alone. This adopted behaviour is violence towards life because it focuses on the denial of life itself.

Many people live under the illusion that if they don't use a weapon or kill then they live a non-violent life, without understanding that the macroscopic scales of violence such as war, genocide and torture are a mere reflection of our internal life in violence. War would simply not manifest if all lived in total acceptance and compassion of their being and life itself. War exists because we are at war with who we are and it will not cease to exist until each one of us takes full responsibility for our internal turmoil and self-violence; until we retrieve our shadow (anti-self) and own it together and in partnership with our luminosity. Each demon you disown becomes a hungry ghost in the world and manifests outside ourselves. Every time you distinguish anger but fail to acknowledge it as your own anger; every time you distinguish greed but fail to accept it as your own greed, and so on, you are unleashing your own shadow into the world and it becomes an external manifestation. You split the darkness out of you because you judge it to be 'bad', and then it leaves, projected onto things and people in the outside.

Distinguishing your own shadow is natural to creation and owning it is accepting a complete picture of who you are. The shadow is not to be feared but embraced and loved. Just as we would hold in our arms a child in fear, we must hold in our arms our anger, fear, jealousy, depression, desire and greed with love and kindness, and understand that our attachment to those states of consciousness comes from our ignorance.

To practice non-violence is to practice impeccability of thought, impeccability of speech and impeccability of action. Reality mirrors our thoughts, speech and actions, and just because they may happen inside of ourselves and other people cannot hear them doesn't mean they have no effect. They all have an effect and generate strong ripples in the ocean of consciousness. Self awareness implies choice of thought, speech and action. As we embrace our darkness and we make it part of our conscious living, we retrieve the capacity to choose our thoughts, speech and actions. This is to strive towards impeccability of doing choosing the ripples we introduce in the ocean.

We know today from quantum mechanics that the universe is an infinite ocean of waves that take form as they are observed. This is no different from the teachings of mysticism and indigenous wisdom. In this ocean of consciousness even the blink of an eye means something. Every time you breathe, feel, or move, the universe breathes, feels and moves with you. The frequency of the ripples that are sent out is determined by the intention of your actions, thoughts and speech, and the same intention will reverberate back to you as the frequency you are sending will find similar frequencies to empathise with.

Do you wonder why life always delivers the same message to you? Maybe it is time to look at the intention with which you are living and understand that the universe is simply talking back at you in your own language. Are you living from greed?, from anger?, from fear?, from love?, from compassion?, or from kindness?

> *The first step of Actualisation of Self is to embrace non-violence in action, speech and thought. Then, as the turmoil in the waters of our existence calm, we can engage consciously in the experience of life and the universe through the Heart.*
>
> # अहिंसा

Ancestral Voices

In order to allow an actualisation that is comprehensive and transpersonal (beyond what I consider personal) it is vital that we incorporate the voices of our ancestors, the voices of indigenous wisdom and mysticism. In the modern world we have left no space for the ancestral myths and wisdom that has been passed down through generations since intelligent life walked this Planet. Even in our recent psychology we consider this information magical, mythical and based on superstition.

Indigenous wisdom is the wisdom that arises from the Earth, meaning the natural universal wisdom that is written in all creation. Indigenous means having sprung from the land, sons and daughters of the soil; intelligent life is simply a more complex form of creation that is part of the unfolding process of the universe. Intelligent life is simply an extension of Pure Being. It is not separate from it nor has it arisen from nothingness.

In the moment life becomes co-creator, and develops the conscious capacity to create, give life and choose, it becomes a mirror reflection of the capacity that lies in consciousness to create and give birth to life. As we immerse ourselves in the illusion of separation and forget about ancestral wisdom and myths, we start believing that we have emerged from nothingness and that we are all that has ever existed, arrogantly believing with our rational mind that we are the centre of the Universe.

We are vessels of Pure Being experiencing another form of existence and, in our capacity to choose, we have responsibility for the effects of our choices. This is a fact that we conveniently prefer to ignore when we live ignorantly.

When we look at the people that inhabit planet Earth today we can easily say that the majority of the world-wide population is of mixed race. After the years we have spent colonising each other and emigrating from one land to another for different reasons depending on the times in history, we have co-created a population of mixed blood, where pure race as such is now very rare. With evolution comes change and we need to welcome our 'pure-race-humanness', rather than keep focusing on our differences; evolving from COLOURness to RAINBOWness.

We are all indigenous to this planet right now; we have all sprung from the land; we are sons and daughters of the soil; and we are all One with creation, with the universe, with the galaxy, with the planet and with one another. According to indigenous wisdom, separation is an illusion and the true reality is that of Pure Being.

People who live in their mind like to ask about the myths and stories of our ancestors: "are they real, do they really exist, or are they simply in the world of spirit?" The answer is that they *are* real, they *do* exist and they *are* in the world of spirit.

In the western style of thinking 'spirit' and 'real' are contradictions, just like we think that 'imagination' and 'fact' are contradictions. Indigenous wisdom, on the other hand, tells us that from Spirit comes true reality, eternal and omnipresent. The notion of separation is the illusion, a relative reality that is impermanent and always has an end. Even the manner in which we ask the question is a contradiction and implies that we believe to be true only that which we can perceive in material form.

The wisdom that has been passed down from our ancestors in words and music is the language of the real realms of Spirit. But today we call it mythology because it appears not to be real if we judge it by material reality. But remember that the imagination is the eye through which we can perceive the true dimensions of being, not the source of hallucinations and delusions emerge.

If a modern psychiatrist with a biological orientation would examine a mystic or a 'medicine person' they could easily label that person as a paranoid schizophrenic because he believes his hallucinations and delusions.

We need to be able to experience the transpersonal reality that surrounds us in order to really *know* that the universe is vibrating energy, waves of possibility. Pure Being. Only personal experience of the realm of Pure Being can bridge the rational thinking into the Heart. This cannot be studied, this can only be lived. The only way to by-pass the mind to allow the Heart to guide us is by practicing a discipline Even if a spontaneous initiation or mystical experience happens to us, it's only the mind that takes the time to integrate such an experience and build a healthy Ego-Self that can then become an expression of that experience and evolve with it, rather than be destroyed by it.

The next section is a change of topic – would you like to put a sub-heading here, such as' Temporality', or 'Understanding Time'
An important aspect of indigenous wisdom is the understanding that time does not exist. Temporality is a perception of the mind. Temporality is the experience that we perceive when the vibratory frequency of phenomena slows down enough to be experienced as a sequence of instants but not enough to be experienced as static. On this Planet we have the gift of temporality and so we can admire the miracle of the growth of nature, animals and beings and also the miracle of the decay of nature, animals and beings. We can almost

trace a line from the beginning of life, through a lifetime to the end of life. But this line is simply an illusory aid that serves the mind to understand and study life. In reality, there is no time-line, no clock ticking the seconds, minutes, hours and years. What we have is the gift of being able to perceive the cycles of creation. From where we are standing, we can see the earth orbiting the Sun and the Solar System moving across the galaxy. According to these cyclic observations, our ancestors created temporality tools that could help them measure and count the movements of creation and evolution. Understanding the cyclic nature of order and chaos inputs and outputs can help us understand the stages that we cross at birth, during life and at death. This is a map of the waves of creation and evolution.

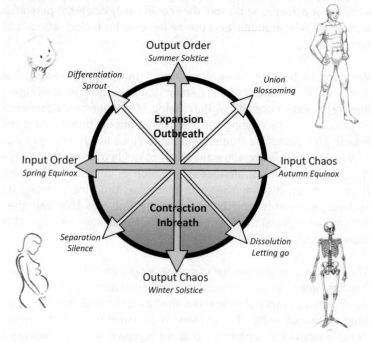

This is a simple calendar cycle that is common to most cultures around the globe. The cycles of the sun, marked by the summer and winter solstice and equinox, and the cycles of the moon, marking the time between each stop of the sun. This is a very basic wheel to measure temporality. Many traditions have their own names for the festivities and they have many other wheels measuring energies; the four weeks of the lunar cycles; long-count calendars; short-count calendars, and so on.

When we look at these cycles, most people who live according to the artificial calendars of the civilized world immediately associate the cycles with agricultural calendars, and often think that they are no longer relevant to our society as many places have evolved from being an agricultural society.

I would ask are we still dependent on the food we grow to survive? I think most people would agree that we are, unless they have become so far removed from the Earth that they believe that frozen synthetic food is all we need to survive. These calendars do not only refer to the cycle of crops growing, which we still depend on, but to the energies that each season and stage represents.

Remember, the Sun is not only a mass of matter. It's an archetypal energy as are the moon and the planets. All that exists is not only matter but Pure Being in different shapes and frequencies. Our mind and bodies physically, causally and astrally, go through these seasons and changes in order to evolve and, no matter how much we choose to deny their influence on us, as far as we are a product of creation, the same energies that affect the galaxy affect us as well.

Embedded in these basic calendar cycles of the sun and the moon we have the basic steps of the perceptual time-line of conception, birth, life, death and rebirth.

These cycles can be observed as a macroscopic reality from the time we are conceived to the time we die, or in a microscopic reality, as every step of the life journey. For example, if we observe only the process of birth, we can find all the stages. At birth we are in union with the mother when the input of chaos triggers labour. As labour starts our environment becomes hostile and we face the dissolution and letting go of the union we had been experiencing so far. The effect, of course, of introducing chaos is output chaos, and as the cervix opens and the birth canal becomes a possible exit for the child, separation becomes imminent as we fight for our life, not knowing what is waiting at the other end. Once we achieve the separation then the Input becomes Order and we are now separate individuals, breathing by ourselves, sprouting into life. As the result of this we have an Output of order that leads us into blossoming or union again.

Every time we enter into order, we experience union and blossoming. Every time we enter into chaos we experience death and separation.

Today, Transpersonal Perinatal Psychology has comprehensive maps that describe the different stages and their ripple effects into our entire life and beyond. From our ancestors we know that the moment of our birth is the moment that we receive the imprint of the purpose of this incarnation. In that manner, what happens during our birth conditions us for life. I don't mean that it traps us for life, it simply conditions. In Indigenous communities, there was a lot of attention placed on birth and death as they clearly understood the two points of entry and exit into the world of phenomena and the separation from Pure Being.

In order to evolve, it is crucial for humanity that we place more importance on conscious conception, birth and death, because the ripple effects of unconscious conception sets in motion a chain of ripples that affect the birth and therefore the lifetime conditioning. If that lifetime is lived in ignorance, it creates turbulent waves that eventually lead to an unconscious death. When we die unconsciously we continue to reincarnate unconsciously, and in that manner we are the single responsible perpetrators of the unconsciousness of suffering and distressed states of consciousness.

These calendars from the Earth and the Universe, from which you can find reference in your own traditions, help us to live in harmony with creation, allowing our being in all its layers to renew itself by engaging consciously in the eternal process of death and birth. In our life this happens constantly: Every day we are born with the dawn and we die at dusk; with every full moon we blossom and with every new moon we die; every year we are born in spring and we die in winter, and so on. This natural miracle of temporality is what makes evolution possible and we are now living in a sacred human body where we are born and die with every in-breath and every out-breath, a miracle not to be missed!

The beginning and the end, birth and death, are crucial points where we can alter the course of evolution towards survival of the human race or keep spiralling towards the extinction of the human race.

Spiritual Sovereignty

When we embrace Pure Being as the absolute reality, we understand that the phenomena we are as human beings is simply a mere reflection of this. We are simply vessels of creative force; transmitters of waves and frequencies from the source.

We are constantly receiving and transmitting information in the form of electromagnetic waves and vibration. But where is the broadcast happening? It is constantly happening as creation unravels from Pure Being into the world of Phenomena.

As separation occurs, different realms take shape and their counterparts form as well; matter and anti-matter always in pairs, Pure Being becoming the one additional variable that enables the balance of matter and anti-matter. Pure Being never dies, so it represents the one extra particle always present and constant to all of creation.

From Pure Being, the realms of light, of sound, of deities and archetypes, angelic forms, dakas and dakinis, all unfold until we find ourselves in human form and, from that point, continue to unravel into different forms of creation, covering the entire spectrum of light and infinite possible frequencies.

We could in very general terms say that the Universe unravels up and down, front and back and left and right, moving in the axis x, y & z, this possibilities provide a simple and complex combination of level of vibratory frequency, evolution or temporality and parallel possibility or dimension which it is always determined by choice.

This can be a simple map of Upper, Middle and Lower realms or a bit more complex like the Tibetan book of life and death suggests or intricate as quantum mechanics.

All possibilities of being exist right here, right now and, at the same time, are simply a reflection of ripples of consciousness that all merge in the One Pure Being. All manifestations are possible because creation has no limits. It is important to remember that, even when experiencing these manifestations of creation, we must never make them solid and confuse them with Pure Being. All that is perceived is an illusion and it must remain, as such, part of the relative reality and experience.

Our spirituality suffered and became controlling religion when we started to solidify these manifestations. When the deities and the gods and goddesses became our truth and reality, we lost connection with spirituality and became slaves of our own illusions.

The sacred scriptures speak about the realms of Spirit that are real, but we forgot the key aspect of creation: all that can be differentiated belongs to the realm of phenomena and is therefore an illusion and must be treated as such. The deities are empty in nature. They are simply archetypal expressions of Pure Being. They can point the way to Pure Being, but they themselves are not Pure Being.

We need to dissolve the solid illusions that we have used as the foundation of a church and religion based on fear and control, to allow the natural flow that has been taught by sages and gurus from every culture and every tradition:

You are IT

You are the Light

You are the Buddha Mind

You are the manifestation (son/daughter) of Pure Being (god)

And yes, there is only ONE son/daughter of Pure Being – YOU. All of the people in your life are reflections in your dream. Can you bear to even imagine that? Can you live accordingly?!

> *To actualise our Spirituality we need to listen to the voices of our ancestors and we have to be free from fear. Only the Heart that is free from fear can enter the room of [mirrors of] Etznab on its death and still love itself unconditionally before it dissolves into the Light; the fearful heart, heavy with guilt and shame will remain trapped in its own hell in Etznab as it will not be able to bare to look at its reflection.*

Socio-Political-Economic Sovereignty

As we continue the journey through our world we encounter our social, political and economic systems. From these realms the actualisation is simple: as the systems have been created by fear and greed, they will only send ripples of fear and greed. A system that has started in ignorance and that has greed at its core, holding it together and making it possible, can never produce equality, harmony or love. It is a system that is designed to control and benefit a few by keeping the majority enslaved by ignorance and numbness.

We can only create systems that will encourage equality and harmony if those in power choose to wake up from their ignorance and embrace their Pure Being essence. Until that happens, a system that is corrupt and twisted cannot suddenly be forced into being honest and genuine.

Until our leaders can see with their own eyes that all around them is simply a reflection of themselves and that we are all an extension of each other, then war will win.

Until our leaders wake up to realise the consequences of their actions and understand that by murdering and discriminating against others they are murdering and discriminating against themselves, violence will own the Planet.

Until our leaders become conscious of their enlightened state and, from that place, rule for the benefit of all beings and the universe, our death sentence as a race will not be lifted.

Would taking the leaders down solve anything? Not if they are taken down with violence and by minds that are lost in fear and greed. All that will happen is a recycling of names and faces but no different result because the input will continue to be fear and greed.

Can change happen in order? No. Chaos needs to occur before a new order is set, just like the cycle of the universal breath dissolution and death needs to happen before a rebirth. If, because of fear, we try to escape 'death' then the change will be unstable and will only create more instability. Only complete dissolution can allow a new order to emerge. Trying to fix a broken machine will only cause more destruction and suffering.

How can we help the change? By finding a way to stop feeding the fear and greed within our own being and outside our being. How can we do this? By finding freedom from suffering, waking up to our own enlightened state. If everyone around you is a reflection in your dream then, if you can wake up to your Pure Being Nature, you will be leading the way and opening the door for all of us in your reflection to find our way into a state of Pure Being.

> *Become Sovereign by learning from your ancestors, experiencing your Pure Being nature and by waking up from ignorance and the nightmare of suffering by practicing Ahimsa - non-violence.*

Health Sovereignty

Our health is not simply the absence of illness but harmonious living. It is important that we understand that health includes allowing space for the natural cycles of life to occur:

Birth, Pain, Illness, Aging and Death

These, as we explored before, are intrinsic qualities of being alive and trying to work against them will only generate suffering. Instead, we need to embrace a model of health that mirrors:

'AIKYA'
harmony, oneness, unity

We can use technology and science in medicine to help human beings to regain harmony when ill and to maintain harmony in their mind and body at a psychical, causal and astral level. We can use our scientific knowledge together with our spiritual wisdom to facilitate the natural flow of life and creation, organically and sustainably. This means that the human being has to be considered in AIKYA as a physical, intellectual and emotional body and mind as well as Pure Being. In this way our medicine enhances healing by helping the individual to regain balance but then it teaches the individual how to maintain balance.

If the system is informed by fear and greed it will be far from producing harmony. Today, thanks to our technological evolution, we can see the immediate results in the body of working with chi, plants, acupuncture and intention. It is vital that these aspects of medicine that have been passed through generations survive and are incorporated into our health model.

Physicians need to actualise their map of the human being so they can treat the whole person and not only separate parts. We need to listen to the medicine and wisdom from the Earth, because we sprung from the Earth and in it we can find all that we need to be in harmony.

When we understand the human being to be multi-dimensional, we need to include the layers of conditioning and karma when looking at an individual, because the ripples that cause illness are vast and are not only related to physical circumstances.

Advances in the medical sciences need to be used for the benefit of all beings and creation and not for profit. We all have the intellectual capacity to be able to weave together a system of Aikya Medicine that can incorporate a variety of healing methods from spirit to physicality in harmony. There is no real difference in the role of a shaman, a psychotherapist or a medical doctor; they all help the person to find wellness and harmony from different perspectives. If they could all could work together, then the person could benefit from a holistic treatment, instead of a partial treatment.

The fields of Psychiatry and Psychology require need to understand the human being in the context of creation. The fields are so split by greed and fear that every approach or 'school of thought' that emerges creates its own new church and a new truth. The practitioners then choose to follow a particular approach as a religion and any alternative view is judged and condemned instead of welcomed.

Whether a method belongs to the Psychoanalytical tradition, the Behavioural, the Humanistic, or Transpersonal is irrelevant. What matters is that each approach does not have to invalidate the others, but rather informs the others. If we look at Freud, Jung, Rogers, Beck, Assaglioli, Wilber, or Grof we could put together a comprehensive _Trans-personal_ *[beyond the personal realms]* perspective of the human being. Welcoming *Aikya*, [harmony, oneness, unity] in psychology and psychiatry is the next leap in evolution. As far as each school of thought remains attached to its COLOURness, the human being will remain stuck in a *split perspective* of its being and therefore of its potential and purpose. The different approaches are only labels to which we attach our identity. If a *mental health* practitioner places so much importance on a label what does that say about their level of consciousness or ignorance? Because if the practitioner feels that the attachment to a label is more important than the well-being of the person, then the practitioner is being incongruent with the very essence of their practice; to help others. Their own ignorance ripples into many homes every time a person hears: *you are mentally ill, there is no cure for your condition, you are chronically depressed, etc*. Again what we see is attachment and fear as the foundation of the system, rather than harmony and equality.

We find the same split when looking at Biology and Quantum Biology, or Physics and Quantum Physics. We like to remain attached to what we know to be true and we make our beliefs our church and religion, condemning all that challenges it. If we are unwilling to let go of our ignorance, no new system will be allowed to emerge. As a collective human race we need to take a leap and actualise ourselves in the fields of medicine, health and well-being according to the ancestral voices and the technological and scientific evolution that we have witnessed. Today, believing that matter is the source of creation, or that depression is a chronic mental disorder, or that health is based on the production of hormones by glands, is as archaic as believing that the earth is flat. We resist change because, in a perverse manner, we're so used to our misery that we have become the guardians of remaining ignorant so change can never happen.

Until health and medical practitioners let go of their attachment to their labels, the systems will be split and will not aid Aikya, harmony or wholeness.
Until health and medical practitioners embrace their Pure Being nature and realise that all around them is a mere reflection of themselves, then the practice will remain in fear and those using the system will suffer because they will be treated only partially, rather than with an Aikya consciousness.

Until health and medical practitioners stop allowing greed to be at the core of their practice, the system will always need illness to survive and not health.

Become Sovereign by taking responsibility for your own sacred mind and body, understanding that the state of Aikya [harmony] can only manifest if you care enough about how you nourish it in physical, intellectual and emotional form.

Voices of Science

The human race has evolved rapidly in the last 100 years, achieving astonishing miracles in science and technology. However, we have used this evolution from greed and fear in wars, violence, expensive drugs, genetically-modified food and exploitation of resources.

We have depleted the Planet from life by using it from ill will and exchanging every inch of forestry for money and concrete. Today we face the imminent extinction of the human race as we spiral into a world of violence, nuclear power and bio-chemical weapons.

All consciousness and voices that have emerged throughout the years, warning us about the misuse of our power, have been ignored, and all the ancestral voices that predicted this possibility have been silenced. This leaves the human race right now, as the calendar of the capitalist world marks 2011 CE, on the edge of extinction.

We have become a virus to the Planet and we have put at risk all life on the Planet by interfering with the natural balance of the Universe. We play with nuclear power without understanding the implications of an atomic explosion in the solar system and the galaxy, or the destruction to life on this planet, and other planets and solar systems.

But on the other hand, we have all the information we need to preserve life. The technological and scientific knowledge we have has the capacity to create sustainable means of producing energy and food, and we have the financial capacity to use the resources of the world to produce equality of living for all. The only catch is, if we try to dream this reality from inside the Grey Spider, from inside the nightmare of fear and greed, it will not work, it will only catapult us into extinction faster. But if we manage to wake up from our ignorant state of greed and fear, then we have a chance.

What we have access today, technologically, can actually help amplify our electromagnetic field and facilitate evolution. There are technologies that can be used to synchronise the brain, train the brain and expand its capacity. Technology can actually help people to reach a state of mind that is expanded beyond the limitations of the world of phenomena.

We are already in the vortex of an evolutionary cycle that will bring change in different forms, where all is sped up and amplified, so if consciously we make use of this vortex to awaken into our Pure

Being nature, then the waves of the change will actually facilitate the change. If, on the other hand, we choose to remain ignorant and decide to continue living in a world of greed and fear then we are simply going to experience an amplified version of greed and fear, nothing new, only bigger and greater.

Until each human being walking the Planet wakes up from ignorance and actualises itself into its Pure Being nature, finding freedom from suffering, then greed has won the battle.

Become an expression of your true nature, find freedom from suffering and engage actively in the change by being present in the best form you can, as an enlightened mind.

DAYA Compassion

As we journey into the realms of our ignorance and our suffering and understand in-depth the implications it has in our lives; when we wake up to the reality of our eternal dance with the 'demons' of greed, anger, jealousy, depression, desire and fear, we can easily get lost in the illusion of suffering. Although we experience this reality in our mind and body, it is not the absolute reality. It is a state of the experience of duality and the world of phenomena. The absolute reality is Pure Being. From the awakened state of Pure Being is where I can witness my individual suffering and struggle. It is from there I can see clearly my limitations, ignorance and attachments to material objects, to beings, to emotions, to thoughts, to behaviours. It is from the seat of the lotus flower that I can truly experience compassion and become compassion. In the moment that I GRANT MYSELF PERMISSION to bear witness to my own suffering and empathise with it in deep sympathy by feeling the extent of my turmoil and my apparent confusion and fear, then just like a loving mother would approach her fearful child, I can open my heart of luminous compassion to gently approach my suffering Ego-Self and slowly hold and bring it close to my Pure Being nature, so that the body in pain can find rest in the rainbow essence of the unconditional love of creation, in the expression of unconditional love that Pure Being represents, in the depth of the compassionate heart of the awakened mind, of the enlightened one, of the luminous one. In the ocean of compassion that I AM.

Compassion is the capacity 'to feel with someone.' It is the capacity to become one and merge with the mind and body that is in suffering in aspiration to find freedom and liberation from that suffering state. Not in the wish of fixing or denying the struggle, because it is precisely because that struggle exists that the mind and body in suffering can end its suffering as the person wakes up from ignorance into their Pure being nature.

The journey into separation and duality gives us the privilege to journey back into the awakened state. The out-breath makes possible the in-breath and vice-versa. All is simply following a beautiful and perfect dance of light and darkness, of Oneness and Separation, of suffering and liberation from suffering. What matters most, what matters only, is the Journey itself, because the destination is always residing within our being and it is called Pure Being.

Compassion is striving to find freedom from our turbulent ignorant state, and is a state of being that every human has and can develop if they GRANT THEMSELVES PERMISSION, if they CHOOSE to.

As we understand compassion in experience and deep meditation, we understand that it is only when we are capable of being compassionate towards ourselves that we can show true compassion to others or the world. When we are focused on displaying compassion as behaviour, or an empty and meaningless practice simply because it is said to be 'good for you', then we are not being compassionate, we are fooling ourselves with the idea of compassion.

Compassion implies full acceptance of who I am in separate form and in united form, as my Ego-Self and as the One. It implies to own my shadow, my darkness, and my demons and to love them as part of who I am by becoming them. When I become my greatest fear, when I realise that the greatest demon to fear is not outside of myself but is myself, then what is there to fear? When I am no longer the victim that is being chased by darkness and demons, but when I can see that I am the darkness and the demon itself, then there is no longer a victim that is afraid and that needs to run and hide.

Practicing compassion also implies that I own my Luminosity and Light, my potential, instead of continuously chasing a god or luminous body outside of myself as if it is a place far away in heaven or a person out of reach. In the moment that I allow myself to own my true nature then there is no longer anywhere to go because I have realised that the great Buddha mind, or Christ essence is me, it has always been me and it will always be me.

From this place of acceptance of the two forces of creation - the great feathered snakes, the sacred couple that emerges from pre-being, I no longer need to be afraid because the demons are me and the angelic beings are me as well. I do not have to wait for a god to forgive me and grant me access to heaven because I am a living expression of heaven; I do not have to fear the demons that reside in hell because I am a living expression of hell. What I have now is CHOICE. As I sit in the lotus seat of Pure Being, darkness and light become the white and black stallions that pull the chariot of my being. I ride the two forces and it is my choice to embrace them and keep them in balance or to let loose one or another and let them become separate of myself. When fearing the Darkness or the Light, I will remain a victim of its force and power, but when their strength is owned and understood as a manifestation of creation that is flowing through the vessel of my being then the victim disappears.

From this understanding I can say that with one hand I have the capacity to love and with the other hand I have the capacity to kill. When, in ignorance, these two stallions are out of control we see people becoming puppets of the forces of violence and anger in complete unconsciousness of their behaviour as it is disguised by their belief that they are 'good' or well-intended.

The compassionate heart knows the consequences of acting out of one force or the other, it sees the karma, the effects, the ripples that energies cause in the cosmos. It knows before it acts the ripples that its thoughts, speech and actions will have, and pauses before taking action, allowing that which will bring benefit to itself and all beings to manifest and that which will bring harm to itself and all beings not to become manifest.

As compassion is the quality that understands and empathises with suffering, once a mind has woken up to its compassionate nature it can stay alert for what can cause it suffering and the paths that lead to suffering. It will, therefore, choose to practice and walk the paths that will help it remain free from suffering. In this manner a compassionate heart does not join the illusion of suffering by serving energies in distress and confusion. Instead, by understanding the universe as a mirror of itself, it owns its own confusion and distress, learns from it, masters it and is no longer afraid of it. The awakened mind in compassion does not eliminate confusion but recognises its own confusion and that is how it frees itself from fear and suffering.

All of these aspects of creation and the universe will remain projections and ghostly aspects of the light and darkness that we chase ferociously and fear greatly until we can grant ourselves permission to become an open heart of compassion, by simply loving and accepting who we are in the aspiration to free ourselves from our suffering.

The final step of Actualisation of Self is to become an active expression of compassion, living in full acceptance of the Self and creation, becoming one with my own suffering and the suffering of others, aspiring to find freedom from it. Be the highest expression of Self love by becoming a Heart of compassion.

The complex and simple practice of Ahimsa and Daya,
of non-violence and compassion
are the algorithms that our human
software needs to actualise.
Becoming a living expression of Ahimsa and Daya
can give PEACE a chance

"The world will little note nor long remember what we say here, but it can never forget what we did here" Abraham Lincoln

"There is always a vast field left to experimentation and I hope that we may have some beautiful progress in the following years" Marie Curie

"No one who believes in non-violence, as a creed, need, therefore, sit still." Mohandas Gandhi

"I believe you can do nothing with hatred...I would like to see a time when man loves his fellow man, and forgets his colour or his creed. We will never be civilized until that time comes" Clarence Darrow

"Beware most strictly of any outbursts of emotion that may endanger needless complications, or any fraternal contention and strife that may create confusion, lead you astray and cause you to lose the confidence of the world" Emperor Hirohito (Showa)

" I have cherished the ideal of a democratic and free society in which all persons live together in harmony and with equal opportunities. It is an ideal which I hope to live for and to achieve. But if needs be, it is an ideal for which I am prepared to die" Nelson Mandela

"The aspiration to peace is...the cornerstone of our pioneering life and labour...To attain peace, I am ready to go at any hour to any place, to meet any authorized leader of any ... state" Golda Meir

"I come here to denounce the two great evils which menace society in general and a society of nations in particular. These two evils are hatred and ignorance" Chaim Herzog

"When I pick up a person from the street, hungry, I give him a plate of rice, a piece of bread, I have satisfied. I have removed that hunger. But a person that is shut out, that feels unwanted, unloved, terrified, the person that has been thrown out from society- that poverty is so hurtful and so much..." Mother Teresa

"We all have become used to the totalitarian system and accepted it as an unchangeable fact and thus helped to perpetuate it. In other words, we are all-though naturally to differing extents-responsible for the operation of the totalitarian machinery; none of us is just a victim, we are all also co-creators." Vaclav Havel

*"The hostile multitudes are vast as space. What chance is there that all should be subdued?
Let but this angry mind be overthrown and every foe is then and there destroyed"* Shantideva

"The loss of memory is the root of oppression" 13th Grandmothers

"Reason is powerless in the expression of Love" Rumi

Chapter XIII
Awakening Consciousness Beyond Yourself

We have been gifted with the miracle of life and as we discover and explore the vastness of reality we discover the vastness of who we are as individuals. Creation is perfect in its imperfection and so are we perfect in our imperfection. As the Universe has unravelled and we have sprung into being as co-creators with the capacity to choose, we have the responsibility to be present to the life we have been given.

All we have is the life we have and that we are living right NOW. All there is, is present moment and we have the capacity to choose right now how we want to live our life.

We only require one input to transform our existence from stuckness and stagnation into flow and growth, and that is the will to change, the wish to 'waken'. If we have no desire to change then nothing will be significantly different in our experience of life as we wake up to another day. But if we have the wish to change and make the life journey a conscious experience of awe and wonder, then suddenly the life that once seemed dull and boring becomes an amazing adventure into the unknown.

We are close to an important transition in the Earth, as the galactic cycles are coming to a cyclic leap and alignment. As we approach 2012, existence as we know it will no longer be. As we saw before all creation has a natural cycle of input and output of order and chaos, just like a cosmic breath that after every out-breath follows an in-breath and, after every in-breath, an out-breath follows again.

Today humanity is passing through a transition from the Input of Chaos that began many years back to the dissolution and letting go of the Output of Chaos, where 'death' and separation are imminent. We can clearly see the themes recreating themselves in our external reality as the systems are no longer infallible; where economies and political regimes are crumbling and changing; where controlling religions and churches are showing signs of internal collapse; where the Earth, in harmony with the energy of the times, is shaking and sneezing. Chaos is a natural stage before any new differentiation and order can occur. Chaos means dissolution, separation, crumbling, collapse, death, anarchy, disorder, but it does not mean 'bad' or 'wrong'.

What is happening is not some sort of divine punishment to the infidels, but simply a natural round of long and short universal cycles. Chaos will take its turn whether we resist it or not and dissolution and death will happen whether we want it or not. In the same manner, order will come again together with differentiation and unity. We are simply in the middle of the cosmic ocean, feeling the waves of evolution and creation - an adventure that is worth living for.

In the middle of this natural cosmic transformation we can certainly make it as painful and horrific as we wish to and we can cause as much harm to each other and the cosmos as we choose to. It will all rise and fall just like waves in the ocean. But what will persevere are the ripples we have left behind, and if the waters that we have left are turbulent and agitated, we will find it very difficult to escape the currents of those waters of suffering and karma. But if we surf the waves of chaos and swim in the depths of the ocean as dissolution and death happens, allowing the universe to do what it knows best how to do, and we simply facilitate and ride the change, then we will not create turbulence in the already chaotic ocean, and as the waves settle we will find it easy to swim and navigate back home where ever home is for you.

Just like any mother giving birth, the cosmos is giving birth and is in labour. The process can be painful and it implies dissolution, separation and death in order for the new life to breathe. So we could question how our actions are helping or creating complications in that cosmic birth:

Are we breathing with the mother?
Are we making her comfortable and reassuring her that all is ok?
Are we speaking to the baby and consciously helping it out?
Are we prepared to receive the baby?

or
Are we shouting and screaming at the mother?
Are we trying to make the pain go away?
Are we trying to stop the baby from coming?
Are we waiting for the forceps?
Are we waiting for the caesarean birth?

Our choices matter and the effects of embracing DAYA and AHIMSA (compassion and non-violence) will reverberate throughout the cosmos of your being and all of creation, creating more DAYA and AHIMSA. Similarly, the effects of embracing the labour and birth in fear, anger and violence will also reverberate throughout the cosmos of your being and all of creation creating more fear, anger and violence.

Birth is imminent. That we cannot change, but how do you want to experience it is entirely your choice and only you will rejoice or suffer for the consequences of your actions and inactions.

The fundamentalist view that this is a biblical apocalypse is simply creating more complications to the birth, and if that is the perspective that you choose to embrace then I have no doubt that you will experience that exact outcome, for after all, the cosmos simply reflects back to us who we are and how we think.

Fear is the great enemy of flow and growth. When we live in fear we control and latch on to absolute truths and beliefs and, even if they prove to be only relative, when in fear we are blind and deaf, so we will not hear. The fear of change itself, the fear of the possibility of chaos will kill many people, not only physically but it will drag them into a bardo of fearfulness after death.

It is out of fear and in extreme circumstances that every human being is capable of anything, even killing; the most horrific actions will take place where fear is king.

Liberation from fear is the personal conquest of death and the genuine understanding that Pure Being never dies and death is simply a transition from one dual experience into another and from phenomena into Pure Being.

> *Conquer death and you will be king in your own kingdom, fear death and you will be forever enslaved in your own kingdom.*

Many speak about a saviour, a messiah that will descend from heaven and will bring those pure of spirit into salvation. This theme is one of the greatest errors of human history. Prophets and enlightened masters have always come into this dimension to help us through difficult times and remind us of what matters most. As we allow greed and fear to cloud humanity in ignorance, we made these great sages into solid churches and controlling religions that could perform our humanly desires for power and conquest in the name of god.

Of course it is true that sages have reincarnated in human form and taught us the ways of light and freedom from suffering, but they have always done it from AHIMSA and DAYA, with humility and simplicity. Today there are many of these great enlightened souls alive on Earth, speaking, to those who have ears to hear and eyes to see, about the ONE to awaken within.

We are very close to a possible public disclosure of intelligent life outside planet Earth and we have technology advanced enough to recreate this biblical and prophetic descent of the one new and only true god. It is a viable possibility today that a light being might descend from the sky, and the big question is:

Am I going to surrender my power to this new, true and only god?

Would it be any different to lose your Sovereignty to a being from another planet, or to a holographic image in the sky than to surrender it to the systems that already have you bound today by fear and control?

If the new being really is the ONE it would be talking to you about becoming Sovereign and embracing your own already enlightened state, not about denying your nature and subordinating you into a new system. To change a Mercedes for a space ship does not make the being coming out of it more enlightened or loving and kind. Only a mind lost in ignorance could make that association.

Maybe it is important to clarify that intelligent life in the cosmos, just like on Earth, has infinite levels of evolution and awakening. Technological supremacy does not equal loving kindness; psychic ability does not equal loving kindness; financial or material wealth does not equal loving kindness. Life can evolve in many forms and shapes and, just as it happens in human form that not all human beings are awakened into enlightenment, other intelligent life is not necessarily awakened into its Pure Being nature.

This is of vital importance to understand as we dive deeper into the evolutionary vortex. As the cosmos is moving, so does the galaxy and so do the planets and stars. Vibratory frequencies are changing and the experience of life is amplifying and speeding up. Human life has been shifting and evolving as the consciousness that incarnates in human form is more advanced and evolved. The result that we see is human beings developing or being born with great psychic capacities, with a collective awareness, and with extremely sensitive receptors to subtle energies. These indigo, crystal and rainbow children and adults are a reality that makes the old science fiction become obsolete, as telepathy, synesthesia, healing, astral projection and intuitive living are natural to them. These qualities have been cultivated by mystics and sages throughout the globe for millennia and today they are not a rare occurrence but a common spontaneous leap of consciousness.

Many indigenous people have spoken about the physical transformation of the human DNA as a parallel occurrence to the cosmic cycles. There is evidence of this happening today but little understanding of the magnitude and implications of this.

Many of these adults and children today are under medication to numb the symptoms of human evolution because they are considered abnormal and displaying maladaptive behaviour. Others are in psychiatric hospitals trying to find an ordinary life in the middle of the chaos that overwhelms them. Many have been diagnosed with autism and ADD while others who have found this world and its violence completely overwhelming have ended their own existence.

But many others have found their way to developing and learning how to moderate and filter the new experiences and abilities. Many are today helping people to heal from cancer and AIDS, providing love and care, hope and faith. These souls have found meaning in their experience like Chiron the wise centaur that was teacher to Asclepiades, Hercules and Apollo. They have understood from their wounds their initiation into a spiritual awakening and have courageously become the hero of their own lives. They have faced death in many faces and human circumstances and they have conquered their fears and risen like the phoenix from the ashes into a luminous existence.

In indigenous wisdom, these types of experiences were considered initiation or rites of passage, where the individual went through difficult circumstances to face their fear of death, so they could conquer it. By becoming the fear and dying we find freedom from the limited perspective of a separate existence and open our doors of perception to a cosmic human experience. As we have disconnected from our mother the Earth, we have forgotten these rites of passage and our societies have become hostile environments for enlightenment and freedom. It is because of this lack of connection that many are unable to find their way through the experience of life, being of a delicate luminous nature. We need to provide our adults and children with context and information that can help them map their experiences as part of the natural collective cosmic evolution that we are experiencing. We need to support and facilitate the flow of the new consciousness emerging rather than wanting it to remain stuck in outdated systems that are suffocating the new life.

On the other hand, as holistic and energy healing has evolved, it is important that we understand that a more advanced body does not automatically equal loving kindness. A person can be a skilled healer or shaman or wizard but it does not mean that because the person is skilled with their energetic and psychic senses that that person is realised and living from loving kindness or Ahimsa or Daya. Many people have approached the new energetic and spiritual healing practices from the same foundation of ignorance and greed. This is important to mention because the result of the consequences of our actions when using these abilities are similar to cutting with a laser instead of cutting with a blunt knife.

This is why you find that in many traditions of mystics and sages certain practices were secret and only taught to the student that was ready to receive them, because it was understood that the consequences that an ability of such kind would cause if used with the intention to harm as opposed to love would be catastrophic.

It is a gift to develop or be born with those capacities, and if we want to make this new consciousness the engine of our leap of evolution we need to embrace the basic understanding that all human life experiences ignorance and that we all meet anger, greed, fear, desire, etc. at different times in different forms. It is only when we deny the existence of these factors that they take possession of our being, making us puppets of their reactions. We all have a shadow and the bigger the light the bigger the shadow, because as far as we are separate phenomena experiencing life in dual form we have a body and mind that creates a shadow and the shadow equals the body and mind that is being reflected. We cannot exorcise our shadow. It is part of who we are, but we can embrace our shadow and, as an awakened mind, allow the two forces, the stallions of the chariot of our being, to gallop in balance and always in front of you.

This new life, this new consciousness, this new baby that is being born, is YOU. The myth of the return of the ONE translates into the awakening into the Pure Being nature that we all are. It is the journey into realisation from a separate existence into a Pure Being consciousness and life. It is the awakening of the dormant life force that resides within the very essence of who you are, the force of the Omecihuatl raising from the Earth, from creation, into the soles of your feet and your spinal channel, travelling upwards into the Heart; the force of Ometecutli descending from the sky into your crown and your spine only to meet its lover, its sacred consort in the Heart, creating a cosmic union that will dissolve the world of Phenomena into the ONE Pure Being nature that you are and have always been and will always be. This is the journey from all directions, from all corners of the universe into the centre, into the promised land beside mount Kailas where a rainbow lake with the White Lotus seat rests; into the land where all sound is the sound of Pure Being and all appearances are empty in nature and radiant in their luminosity, to the promised land of Paititi, the city of golden light.

This is the final stop, where all rests in peace and emptiness. This is the journey of AWAKENING CONSIOUSNESS beyond yourself into your Pure Being state. The journey of conquering death and embracing the serpent force of the feathered dragons that give birth to all of creation, not outside of you but within you; the journey of dissolution from duality into unity, from separation into oneness.

You are the ONE
Awakening Consciousness

"...When dusk came Tule cried, as he knew himself to be one with the sacred feathered-dragons, performing the dance of Light and Darkness in a magnificent display of rainbow colours.

When night and rest came Tule closed his eyes to the outside and silenced with Lotus inside...only to hear one last teaching...

"...there is no Lotus, so don't take it all too seriously!"

Namaste
Ná Áak

Contribution from Stanislav Grof,M.D., Ph.D.

Archetypes, Mythic Imagination, and Modern Society.

I will begin this paper on the importance of mythic imagination and archetypal psychology for modern society with a brief discussion of the nature and function of the archetypes and how our understanding of them has changed over the centuries. Following this, I will address more specifically the implications of archetypal thinking for a variety of disciplines and its relevance for the global crisis we are currently facing.

According to the understanding that has emerged from Jungian psychology, consciousness research, and scholarly mythological research, archetypes are timeless primordial cosmic principles underlying, informing, and forming the fabric of the material world (Jung 1959). The tendency to interpret the world in terms of archetypal principles first appeared in ancient Greece and was one of the most striking characteristics of Greek philosophy and culture.

As Richard Tarnas pointed out in his sequel to The Passion of the Western Mind entitled Psyche and Cosmos: Intimations of a New World View (Tarnas 1993), archetypes can be seen from several different perspectives:

1. In Homeric epics they took the form of <u>personified mythological figures</u>, as deities, such as Zeus, Poseidon, Dionysos, Hera, Aphrodite, or Ares.

2. In the philosophy of Plato, they were described as <u>pure metaphysical principles</u>, transcendent Ideas or Forms. They possessed independent existence of their own in a realm not accessible to ordinary human senses. According to him, earthly things partake in the shape or character of these universal Forms or Ideas, but they fall far short of the

perfect glory or perfect reality of these transcendent Forms/Ideas (Plato 1961).

3. In modern times, C. G. Jung brought the concept of archetypes into modern psychology, describing them primarily as <u>psychological principles</u>.

The existence of hidden invisible dimensions of reality is an idea that is alien to materialistic science, unless these are material in nature and can be made accessible through the use of devices that extend the range of our senses, such as microscopes, telescopes, or sensors detecting various bands of electromagnetic radiation. In addition, academic and clinical psychiatrists use a very narrow conceptual framework that limits the human psyche to postnatal biography and the Freudian individual unconscious.

According to them, the experiences of archetypal beings and realms are not ontologically real; they are figments of human imagination or pathological products of the brain that require treatment by tranquilizing medication.

Modern materialistic science thus joined the centuries old philosophical argument between the *nominalists* and *realists* and emphatically decided in favor of the in favour of the former. The debate between the nominalists and realists permeated in its many variations the entire history of Western philosophy nominalists. The nominalists saw the archetypes as "names," abstractions from human experience of concrete objects and situations and thus derivatives of the material world. The realists believed that the archetypal world is ontologically real, although not accessible to human senses. It was the clinical and philosophical work of C. G. Jung that radically changed this situation.

Jung's analysis of the dreams and symptoms of his clients, as well as his study of world mythology, art, comparative religion, and ritual life of native cultures brought convincing evidence for the existence of the collective unconscious and for ontological reality of the archetypes as its governing principles (Jung 1959). However, Jung's understanding of the nature and function of archetypes changed dramatically in the course of his life. In his early work, he saw them as transindividual but essentially intrapsychic phenomena. He believed that they were hard-wired into the human brain and often compared them with instincts.

It was the observation of a phenomenon that Jung called *synchronicity* that radically changed his perspective on archetypes (Jung 1960). He observed that everyday life often brings striking coincidences that by far transcend any reasonable probability; they should not happen if the universe were governed exclusively by chains of causes and effects. He cited as examples the work of the Austrian biologist Kammerer and Flammarion's story of the rare plum pudding. Moreover, he observed that in many of these coincidences intrapsychic events form meaningful patterns with material reality (Jung's scarab, Campbell's praying mantis, my When the Impossible Happens). This would be possible only if archetypes were cosmic organizing principles governing the human psyche, as well as material reality.

Joseph Campbell's comparative studies of mythology brought strong supportive evidence for Jung's understanding of archetypes and represent an important complement to and support for his clinical explorations. Of particular interest in this regard is Campbell's crosscultural study of the archetypal motif of the Hero's Journey that he referred to as "monomyth" because of its universal and ubiquitous nature transcending historical and geographical boundaries. He first described this motif in his 1947 classic The Hero with A Thousand faces (Campbell 1968) and later demonstrated how it manifests in a variety of situations including the shamanic initiatory crisis, experiences in rites of passage, mysteries of death and rebirth, and in psychoses.

Additional validation of the ontological reality of archetypes came from psychedelic therapy and powerful non-drug experiential techniques (Grof 1985 and 2000).

Implications of the new understanding:

1. Archetypes in Psychiatry, Psychology, and Psychotherapy:

In the light of the observations from psychedelic therapy and the work with holotropic breathwork, the cartography of the psyche used by academic psychiatry and psychology, which is limited to postnatal biography and to the Freudian individual unconscious, has to be vastly expanded. It has to include the perinatal domain and the transpersonal domain – particularly the collective unconscious with its archetypal dynamics (Grof 1985, 2000). Modern consciousness research has shown that in nonordinary states archetypes can be directly experienced and bring new information about mythologies of the world unknown to the subject (Jung's example of the chronic psychotic patient – sun making wind with the movements of its penis as in Mithraic mythology).

To illustrate this, I would like to describe one of many situations in which the authenticity of such information could be verified.

It involved one of my clients in Prague, whom I treated for depression and pathological fear of death (*thanatophobia*). In one of his psychedelic sessions, he experienced a powerful sequence of psychospiritual death and rebirth. As the experience was culminating, he had a vision of an ominous entrance into the underworld guarded by a terrifying pig goddess. At this point, he suddenly felt an urgent need to draw a specific geometrical design and asked me to bring him some sheets of paper and drawing utensils. He drew an entire series of complex abstract patterns and he kept impulsively tearing and crumpling these intricate designs as soon as he finished them. He was very dissatisfied with his drawings and was getting increasingly frustrated, because he was not able to 'get it right'.

At that time, I was still under a strong influence of my Freudian training and I tried my best to identify the unconscious motives for this strange behavior by using the method of free associations. We spent much time on this task, but without much success. The entire sequence simply did not make any sense. Eventually, the process moved to other areas and I stopped thinking about this situation. The entire episode had remained for me completely mysterious until many years later, when I moved to the United States.

During our stay at Esalen, Joseph Campbell frequently conducted workshops there and participated as guest faculty in many of our month long seminars. In the middle of the week, he regularly came for dinner in our house, because he became tired of the Esalen menu, which he called "rabbit food." We had many fascinating discussions over the years, during which I shared with him various observations of obscure archetypal experiences from my work that I was not able to understand. In most instances, Joseph had no difficulties identifying the cultural sources of the symbolism involved.

During one of these discussions, I remembered the above episode and shared it with him. "How fascinating," said Joseph without any hesitation, "it was clearly the Cosmic Mother Night of Death, the Devouring Mother Goddess of the Malekulans in New Guinea." He then continued to tell me that the Malekulans believed they would encounter this deity during the Journey of the Dead. She had the form of a frightening female figure with distinct pig features. According to the Malekulan tradition, she sat at the entrance into the underworld and guarded an intricate sacred labyrinthine design.

The Malekulans had an elaborate system of rituals that involved breeding and sacrificing pigs. This complex ritual activity was aimed at overcoming the dependency on their human mothers and eventually on the Devouring Mother Goddess. The Malekulans spent an enormous amount of time practicing the art of the labyrinth drawing, since its mastery was considered essential for a successful journey to the Beyond. Joseph, with his lexical knowledge, was able to solve an important part of this puzzle that I had come across during my research. The remaining question, that even he was not able to answer, was why my client had to encounter specifically this Malekulan deity at that particular time of his therapy. However, the task of mastering the posthumous journey certainly made good sense for somebody whose main symptom was pathological fear of death.

Of the many experiences involving the archetypal world I have myself had in my psychedelic sessions, the most interesting one happened in a session with MDMA.

In the first part of this session, I experienced scenes of unimaginable destruction. Scenes of natural disasters – volcanic eruptions, earthquakes, crashing meteors, tidal waves, forest fires and floods were combined with images of exploding atomic bombs, burning cities, collapsing highrise buildings, and horrors of wars. Heading this wave of total annihilation were four terrifying horsemen, I realized that I was experiencing the archetype of the Apocalypse. This experience coincided with a stage in my spiritual development when I recognized the illusory nature of the material world and started seeing it as a play of Cosmic Consciousness – lila.

In the final sequence of the session, I had a vision of a large brilliantly lit stage that was located somewhere beyond time and space. It had a beautiful ornate curtain decorated with intricate patterns that seemed to contain the entire history of the world. I intuitively understood that I was visiting the Theatre of the Cosmic Drama, featuring the forces that shape human history. I began to witness a magnificent parade of mysterious figures who entered the stage, presented themselves, and slowly departed.

I realized that what I was seeing were personified universal principles, archetypes, that through a complex interplay create the illusion of the phenomenal world, the divine play that the Hindus call lila. They were protean personages condensing many identities, many functions, and even many scenes. As I was watching them, they kept changing their forms in extremely intricate holographic interpenetration, being one and many at the same time. I was aware that they had many different facets, levels, and dimensions of meaning, but was not able to focus on anything in particular.

Each of these figures seemed to represent simultaneously the essence of his or her function, as well as all the concrete manifestations of the principle they represented. There was Maya, the magical ethereal figure symbolizing the world illusion, Anima, embodying the eternal Female, the Warrior, a Mars-like personification of war and aggression, the Lovers, representing all the sexual dramas and romances throughout ages, the royal figure of the Ruler or Emperor, the withdrawn Hermit, the facetious and elusive Trickster, and many others. As they were passing across the stage, they bowed in my direction, as if expecting appreciation for their stellar performance in the divine play of the universe.

The work with non-ordinary states of consciousness (their important subgroup that I call "holotropic") has shown beyond any reasonable doubt that archetypal experiences are not erratic products of brain pathology of unknown origin (symptoms of "endogenous psychoses"), but creations of anima mundi emerging into individual consciousness (Grof 2000). It has also revealed the existence of the perinatal domain in the unconscious that contains a unique mixture of fetal and archetypal elements. This has profound theoretical and practical implications for psychiatry, psychology, and psychotherapy:

a. Archetypes play an important role in the genesis of emotional and psychosomatic symptoms as part of multilevel dynamic systems that consist of biographical, perinatal, and transpersonal material (COEX systems). Conversely, archetypes can also play an important role in healing and transformation (the extreme being emergence and integration of a demonic archetype)

b. This is closely related to inner healing intelligence of the psyche (Jung's individuation process) and healing potential of archetypal figures or cosmic energy that ancient and native cultures see as divine (Apollo of the Greek temple incubation, deities of the Caribbean and South American syncretistic religions – the loa in Voodoo or orishas in Umbanda and Santeria, pneuma of the Gnostics, prana of Kundalini Yoga, ntum of the Kalahari Bushmen, mana of the Polynesians, etc.)

c. The discovery of the ontological reality of the archetypal realm and the inner healing intelligence supports the concept of "spiritual emergency" (emergence of Perinatal and transpersonal material into consciousness) as an alternative to the medical understanding of "endogenous psychoses" as mental diseases, caused by a pathological process (Grof and Grof 1989, Grof and Grof 1991).

2. The Role of Archetypes in Science:

a. Archetypes play an important role in the genesis of scientific theories and in scientific discoveries. As Phillipp Frank has shown in his book Philosophy of Science (1957), the source of the basic axiom of a scientific theory or the source of a scientific discovery is often an archetypal motif. In the history of science revolutionary ideas often emerge long before there is sufficient evidence to justify them or support them. Examples are the Ionic philosopher Anaximandros with his protoevolutionary theory suggesting that all life originated in the ocean, Demokritos and Leukippos with their atomic theory of matter, Copernicus and Kepler who drew their inspiration from the solar archetype, Friedrich Kekule inspired by the vision of Uroboros in his discovery of the benzene ring, Einstein's preoccupation with the unified theory, etc.

b. There is also increasing awareness of the importance of archetypal patterns in various scientific disciplines: Goethe's fascination by the building plan of plants, Gregory Bateson's preoccupation with the "pattern that connects" in nature and with evolutionary theory, Sheldrake's concept of morphogenetic fields, Ilya Prigogine's theory of dissipative structures, chaos theory, etc.

3. Archetypes, Religion, and Spirituality:

The discovery that the archetypal world is ontologically real gives legitimacy to the spiritual worldview, spiritual quest, and to religious activity that involves direct experience. It makes it possible to distinguish organized religions based on belief, with their dogmas, ritualism, moralism, and secular ambitions, from authentic spirituality found in the monastic and mystical branches of religions and in groups emphasizing spiritual practice and direct experience.

Spirituality is based on direct experiences of non-ordinary aspects and dimensions of reality. It does not require a special place or an officially appointed person mediating contact with the divine. The mystics do not need churches or temples. The context in which they experience the sacred dimensions of reality, including their own divinity, are their bodies and nature. And instead of officiating priests, they need a supportive group of fellow seekers or the guidance of a teacher who is more advanced on the inner journey than they are themselves.

Another important distinction to make is the difference between idolatry and mysticism; According to Joseph Campbell (echoing Karlfried Graf Durckheim), "a useful deity (archetypal figure) has to be transparent to the transcendent;" it has to point to the Absolute, but not be mistaken for it. Making the archetypal figure opaque and worshipping it as the ultimate is idolatry; it results in a religion that unites within its radius, but divides the world into rival groups - Christians/pagans, Moslems/infidels, Jews/goyim.

The realization of the ontological reality of the archetypal world validates the ritual and spiritual life of pre-industrial cultures – shamanism, rites of passage, mysteries of death and rebirth, and the great religions and spiritual philosophies of the East and West. Of these, rites of passage are of particular importance for modern society. According to scholars, such as Margaret Mead and Mircea Eliade the fact that the industrial civilization has lost meaningful rites of passage contributes significantly to the ills of modern society, particularly of the young generation – sexual acting out, drug abuse, and violence.

Margaret Mead and Catherine Bateson organized in 1973 a small working conference in Burg Wartenstein in Austria, entitled Ritual, Reconciliation in Change. Several years ago, Christina's attended a conference, convened by a New York state legislator on the same subject – importance of rites of passage and the possibility of recreating and reinstituting them. Participants discussed the possibility of combining such elements as ropes courses, outward bound, fire walking, and Holotropic breathwork (since all native rites of passage involve non-ordinary states of consciousness). The authors of the strategic doctrine refer to members of their community as the "nuclear priesthood," the first atomic test was called Trinity – the unity of Father, Son, and Holy Ghost, the male forces of creation. The scientists who worked on the **atomic bomb** and witnessed the test described it in the following way: **"It was as though we stood at the first day of creation."** And Robert Oppenheimer thought of Krishna's words to Arjuna in the Bhagavad Gita: "I am become Death, the Shatterer of Worlds."

4. Archetypes and Sociopolitical Movements in History:

Archetypal forces govern not only processes in the individual psyche, but also in the collective psyche, they are forces of history. Medieval knights were asked to sacrifice their lives for Jesus and participate in the Crusades to recover the Holy Land from the Mohammedans. The Bohemian Hussites called themselves "Warriors of God" and sung their powerful chorale "Ye Who Are the Warriors of God" with such intensity that it allegedly wreaked havoc among the enemies they were about to engage and made them flee the battlefield. Hitler used archetypal symbols to influence his followers – the Vedic images of the swastika and the solar eagle, the Thousand Years' Reich, and the supremacy of the Nordic race.

C. G. Jung noticed that the archetypal motif of Ragnarok (Goetterdaemmerung or Twilight of the Gods) kept appearing in the dreams of his German patients. He concluded that Germany was facing a national catastrophe and that it would be destructive and self-destructive in nature. He also analyzed the archetypal aspects of Hitler and Stalin (Jung 1950) and discussed the political implications of the Wotan archetype for Germany (Jung 1964). Marie-Louise von Franz discussed in her article The Transformed Berserk the importance of the experience of Nikolas von Flue, the patron saint of Switzerland (his vision of the Wotanic Christ), for the future of her homeland (Franz 1988). James Hillman amassed in his brilliant book A Terrible Love of War convincing evidence that war is a formidable archetypal force that has irresistible power over individuals and nations (Hillman 2004).

Ronald Reagan made in his speeches references to the Apocalypse and called the Soviet Union the "Evil Empire." George Bush called his fight against Moslem terrorists a "crusade"; in turn, Moslem extremists use for political purposes the concept of jihad, the Holy War against the infidels, and Moslem terrorists' expect as reward for their suicidal attacks on infidels the delights of Paradise, including the virginal black-eyed houris. Similarly the Japanese kamikaze warriors in the Second World War believed that they sacrificed their life for the living god – "Emperor of Heaven" Hirohito.

The authors of the strategic doctrine refer to members of their community as the "nuclear priesthood." The first atomic test was called Trinity -- the unity of Father, Son, and Holy Ghost. The scientists who worked on the atomic bomb and witnessed the test described it in the following way: "It was as though we stood at the first day of creation." And Robert Oppenheimer thought of Krishna's words to Arjuna in the Bhagavad Gita: "I am become Death, the Shatterer of Worlds."

Work with holotropic states of consciousness, with and without psychedelics offers fascinating insights into the archetypal and perinatal roots of war and bloody revolution, The images of violent sociopolitical events typically accompany the reliving of biological birth and appear in very specific connection with the consecutive stages of the birth process (BPMs). Each stage is connected with specific archetypal imagery mixed with corresponding fetal elements (Grof 1985, 2000).

While we are reliving episodes of undisturbed intrauterine existence (BPM I), we typically experience images from human societies where people live in harmony with each other and with nature. The archetypal domain contributes images of paradises and heavens of various cultures, Disturbing intrauterine memories, such as those of a toxic womb, imminent miscarriage, or attempted abortion, are accompanied by images of human groups living in industrial areas where nature is polluted and spoiled, or in societies with insidious social order and all-pervading paranoia. Corresponding archetypal images feature insidious demons.

Typical archetypal images associated with the onset of delivery are ominous whirlpools, engulfing or constricting monsters (dragon, Leviathan, whale, Tarantula, octopus), or entries into the underworld. Regressive experiences related to the first clinical stage of birth (BPM II), during which the uterus periodically contracts but the cervix is not open, present a very characteristic picture. They portray oppressive and abusive totalitarian societies with closed borders, victimizing their populations, and "choking" personal freedom, such as Czarist or Communist Russia, Hitler's Third Reich, South American dictatorships, and the African Apartheid), or bring specific images of the inmates in Nazi concentration camps and Stalin's Gulag Archipelago. While experiencing these scenes of living hell, we identify exclusively with the victims and feel deep sympathy for the downtrodden and the underdog. Underlying all these is the archetype of hell – extreme physical and emotional suffering that will never end, complete with the images of devils and sinners.

The experiences accompanying reliving of the second clinical stage of delivery (BPM III), when the cervix is dilated and continued contractions propel the fetus through the narrow passage of the birth canal, feature a rich panoply of violent scenes – bloody wars and revolutions, human or animal slaughter, mutilation, sexual abuse, and murder. These scenes often contain demonic elements and repulsive scatological motifs. Additional frequent concomitants of BPM III are visions of fire - burning cities, launching of rockets, and explosions of nuclear bombs. Here we are not limited to the role of victims, but can participate in three roles - that of the victim, of the aggressor, and of an emotionally involved observer. When the third matrix approaches resolution, the archetypal images feature figures representing death and rebirth, such as Osiris, Dionysus, Quetzalcoatl, Inanna, or Jesus, Phoenix, or deities associated with fire (Moloch, Pele).

The events characterizing the third clinical stage of delivery (BPM IV), the actual moment of birth and the separation from the mother, are typically associated with images of victory in wars and revolutions, liberation of prisoners, and success of collective efforts, such as patriotic or nationalistic movements. At this point, we can also experience visions of triumphant celebrations and parades or of exciting postwar reconstruction.

Archetypal motifs that belong here are rainbow spectra, peacock designs, Great Mother Goddesses, and images of deities appearing in light (angelic beings, gandharvas and apsaras, etc.)

In 1975, I described these observations, linking sociopolitical upheavals to stages of biological birth, in Realms of the Human Unconscious (Grof 1975). Shortly after its publication, I received a letter from Lloyd de Mause, a New York psychoanalyst and journalist. De Mause is one of the founders of psychohistory, a discipline that applies the findings of depth psychology to history and political science (Mause 1975).

Psychohistorians study such issues as the relationship between the childhood history of political leaders and their system of values and process of decision-making, or the influence of child-rearing practices on the nature of revolutions of that particular historical period. Lloyd de Mause was very interested in my findings concerning the trauma of birth and its possible sociopolitical implications, because they provided independent support for his own research.

For some time, de Mause had been studying the psychological aspects of the periods preceding wars and revolutions. It interested him how military leaders succeed in mobilizing masses of peaceful civilians and transforming them practically overnight into killing machines. His approach to this problem was very original and creative. In addition to analysis of traditional historical sources, he drew data of great psychological importance from caricatures, jokes, dreams, personal imagery, slips of the tongue, side comments of speakers, and even doodles and scribbles on the edge of the rough drafts of political documents. By the time he contacted me, he had analyzed in this way seventeen situations preceding the outbreak of wars and revolutionary upheavals, spanning many centuries since antiquity to most recent times.

He was struck by the extraordinary abundance of figures of speech, metaphors, and images related to biological birth that he found in this material. Military leaders andpoliticians of all ages describing a critical situation or declaring war typically used terms that equally applied to perinatal distress. They accused the enemy of choking and strangling their people, squeezing the last breath out of their lungs, or constricting them and not giving them enough space to live (Hitler's "Lebensraum"). We could illustrate this by a recent example – Osama bin Laden threatening in his videotape that he would turn United States into a "choking hell."

Equally frequent were allusions to dark caves, tunnels, and confusing labyrinths, dangerous abysses into which one might be pushed, and the threat of engulfment by treacherous quicksand or a terrifying whirlpool. Similarly, the offer of the resolution of the crisis comes in the form of perinatal images. The leader promises to rescue his nation from an ominous labyrinth, to lead it to the light on the other side of the tunnel, and to create a situation where the dangerous aggressor and oppressor will be overcome and everybody will again "breathe freely."

Lloyd de Mause's historical examples at the time included such famous personages as Alexander the Great, Napoleon, Samuel Adams, Kaiser Wilhelm II., Hitler, Khrushchev, and Kennedy. Samuel Adams talking about the American Revolution referred to "the child of Independence now struggling for birth." In 1914, Kaiser Wilhelm stated that "the Monarchy has been seized by the throat and forced to choose between letting itself be strangled and making a last ditch effort to defend itself against attack."

During the Cuban missile crisis Krushchev wrote to Kennedy, pleading that the two nations not "come to a clash, like blind moles battling to death in a tunnel."

Even more explicit was the coded message used by Japanese ambassador Kurusu when he phoned Tokyo to signal that negotiations with Roosevelt had broken down and that it was all right to go ahead with the bombing of Pearl Harbor. He announced that the "birth of the child was imminent" and asked how things were in Japan: "Does it seem as if the child might be born?" The reply was: "Yes, the birth of the child seems imminent."

Interestingly, the American intelligence listening in recognized the meaning of the "waras-birth" code.

Particularly chilling was the use of perinatal language in connection with the explosion of the atomic bomb in Hiroshima. The airplane was given the name of the pilot's mother, Enola Gay, the atomic bomb itself carried a painted nickname "The Little Boy," and the agreed-upon message sent to Washington as a signal of successful detonation was "The baby was born." It would not be too far-fetched to see the image of a newborn also behind the nickname of the Nagasaki bomb, Fat Man. Since the time of our correspondence, Lloyd de Mause collected many additional historical examples and refined his thesis that the memory of the birth trauma plays an important role as a source of motivation for violent social activity.

The issues related to nuclear warfare are of such relevance that I would like to elaborate on them using the material from a fascinating paper by Carol Cohn entitled "Sex and Death in the Rational World of the Defense Intellectuals" (Cohn 1987). The defense intellectuals (DIs) are civilians who move in and out of government, working sometimes as administrative officials or consultants, sometimes at universities and think tanks. They create the theory that informs and legitimates U.S. nuclear strategic practice - how to manage the arms race, how to deter the use of nuclear weapons, how to fight a nuclear war if the deterrence fails, and how to explain why it is not safe to live without nuclear weapons. Carol Cohn had attended a two-week summer seminar on nuclear weapons, nuclear strategic doctrine, and arms control. She was so fascinated by what had transpired there that she spent the following year immersed in the almost entirely male world of defense intellectuals (except for secretaries). She collected some extremely interesting facts confirming the perinatal dimension in nuclear warfare. In her fascinating paper, she mentions eight historical examples, where coded messages and other communications about development and testing of atomic and hydrogen bombs involved references to birth and newborns.

Further support for the pivotal role of the perinatal domain of the unconscious in war psychology can be found in Sam Keen's excellent book The Faces of the Enemy (Keen 1988). Keen brought together an outstanding collection of distorted and biased war posters, propaganda cartoons, and caricatures from many historical periods and countries.

He demonstrated that the way the enemy is described and portrayed during a war or revolution is a stereotype that shows only minimal variations and has very little to do with the actual characteristics of the country and culture involved.

He was able to divide these images into several archetypal categories according to the prevailing characteristics (e.g., Stranger, Aggressor, Worthy Opponent, Faceless, Enemy of God, Barbarian, Greedy, Criminal, Torturer, Rapist, Death). According to Keen, the alleged images of the enemy are essentially projections of the repressed and unacknowledged shadow aspects of our own unconscious. Although we would certainly find in human history instances of just wars, those who initiate war activities are typically substituting external targets for elements in their own psyches that should be properly faced in personal self-exploration.

Sam Keen's theoretical framework does not specifically include the Perinatal domain of the unconscious. However, the analysis of his picture material reveals preponderance of archetypal images that are characteristic of BPM II and BPM III. The
enemy is typically depicted as a dangerous octopus, a vicious dragon, a multiheaded hydra, a giant venomous tarantula, or an engulfing Leviathan. Other frequently used symbols include vicious predatory felines or birds, monstrous sharks, and ominous snakes, particularly vipers and boa constrictors. Scenes depicting strangulation or crushing, ominous whirlpools, and treacherous quicksands also abound in pictures from the time of wars, revolutions, and political crises. Juxtaposition of pictures from holotropic states of consciousness that depict perinatal experiences with the historical pictorial documentation collected by Lloyd de Mause and Sam Keen represents strong evidence for the perinatal and transpersonal roots of human violence.

According to the new insights, provided jointly by observations from consciousness research and the findings of psychohistory, we all carry in our deep unconscious powerful energies and emotions associated with the trauma of birth that we have not adequately mastered and assimilated. The symbolism associated with them is drawn from deep archetypal sources. For some of us, this aspect of our psyche can be completely unconscious, until and unless we embark on some in-depth self-exploration with the use of psychedelics or some powerful experiential techniques of psychotherapy, such as the holotropic breathwork or rebirthing. Others can have varying degrees of awareness of the emotions and physical sensations from the perinatal and transpersonal level of the unconscious.

Activation of this material can lead to serious individual psychopathology, including unmotivated violence. It seems that, for unknown reasons, the awareness of the perinatal elements can increase simultaneously in a large number of people. This creates an atmosphere of general tension, anxiety, and anticipation. The leader is an individual who is under a stronger influence of the perinatal energies than the average person. He also has the ability to disown his unacceptable feelings (the Shadow in Jung's terminology) and to project them on the external situation. The collective discomfort is blamed on the enemy and a military intervention is offered as a solution.

Historical and astrological research of Richard Tarnas threw fascinating new light on de Mause's idea of the collective tension originating in the perinatal unconscious which typically precedes onset of wars and revolutions. In his meticulous explorations, Tarnas recognized the deep correlation between the phenomenology of what I call Basic Perinatal Matrices (BPMs) and astrological archetypes (BPM I and Neptune, BPM II and Saturn, BPM III, and Pluto and BPM IV and Uranus). He also was able to demonstrate throughout human history deep correlations between the periods of wars and revolutions and hard Pluto/Saturn aspects (Tarnas 2006).

5. Search for a New Planetary Myth.

Scholars, such as Arnold Toynbee and Joseph Campbell noticed that all cultures of the past were governed by an underlying myth or a combination of myths. Joseph Campbell often raised the question: "What are the myths that are driving the Western civilization?" He himself emphasized the importance of the Search for the Holy Grail myth in its relation to individualism characterizing Western society. We can also think about the two major myths of the modern era: Paradise Lost vs. Ascent of Man. Equally appropriate seems to be the motif of the Abduction and Rape of the Feminine, Death/Rebirth Struggle, and a variety of others - Faust, Sorcerer's Apprentice, Frankenstein, Prodigal Son, Tower of Babel, etc.

Joseph Campbell also often asked: what will be the myth of the future and he expressed his hope that it would
involve overcoming fragmentation and creating a planetary civilization, where people would live in harmony with others and with nature, benefiting from the astonishing discoveries of science and technology, but using them with wisdom coming from a deep spiritual place (New Atlantis). Achievement of this goal would also involve psychospiritual rebirth and liberation and return of the feminine.

Since we are talking about planetary civilization, I would like to mention a very interesting observation that seems very relevant in this regard. One of the most surprising discoveries in my work with psychedelics and with the holotropic Breathwork was the ease with which individuals in holotropic states of consciousness (including myself) transcended historical and geographical boundaries and experienced archetypal figures, motifs, and domains from just about any culture in human history. Over the years, I have myself have experienced in my own psychedelic sessions episodes from many different mythologies and religions of the world – Hindu, Buddhist, Tibetan Buddhist, Moslem, Christian, Egyptian, Shinto, Australian Aborigene, Native American, South American, and others.

This has to be a new phenomenon. Many other cultures had and used powerful mind-altering technologies, including psychedelic plants. Had the collective unconscious in its entirety been as easily accessible for them as it seems to be for modern subjects, we would not have distinct culture-specific mythologies. We have to assume that, for example, the Tibetans experienced primarily Tibetan deities and Huichol Indians in Mexico Huichol deities. There are no descriptions of the Dear Spirit or Grandfather Fire in the Bardo Thodol or those of the Dhyani Buddhas in the Huichol lore.

It seems that this increased accessibility of various domains in the collective unconscious parallels what is happening in the material world. Until the end of the fifteenth century, Europeans did not know anything about the New World and its inhabitants and vice versa. Many human groups in remote parts of the world remained unknown to the rest of the world until the modern era. Tibet was relatively isolated until the Chinese invasion in 1949. Today telephone, short-wave radio stations, television, jet travel, and more recently the Internet have dissolved many of the old boundaries. Let us hope that what is happening in the inner and the outer world are indications that we are moving toward a truly global civilization.

6. Consciousness research, archetypal psychology, and astrology.

The new understanding of the nature and function of the archetypes that has emerged from the study of holotropic states of consciousness has important implications for the field of astrology. On the one hand, it brings strong supportive evidence for the worldview underlying astrology (Grof 2009), on the other hand it opens new exciting perspectives for psychiatry, psychology, and a broad range of other disciplines. This is a complex topic that has to be reserved for another time and place.

Bibliography:
Campbell, J. 1968. The Hero with A Thousand Faces. Princeton: Princeton University Press.

Cohn, C. 1987. "Sex and Death in the Rational World of the Defense Intellectuals." Journal of Women in Culture and Society 12:687-718.

Frank, P. 1957. Philosophy of Science, Englewood-Cliffs, N.J.: Prentice Hall.

Franz, M. L. von. 1988. "The Transformed Berserk." In: Grof, S. (ed.): Human

Survival and Consciousness Evolution. Albany, NY: State University of New York (SUNY) Press.

Grof, S. 1975. Realms of the Human Unconscious: Observations from LSD Research. New York: Viking Press. Paperback: E. P. Dutton, New York, 1976.

Grof, S. 1985. Beyond the Brain: Birth, Death, and Transcendence in Psychotherapy. Albany, NY: State University of New York (SUNY) Press.

Grof, S. 2000. Psychology of the Future: Lessons from Modern Consciousness Research. Albany, NY: State University of New York (SUNY) Press.

Grof, C. and Grof, S. 1991. The Stormy Search for the Self: A Guide to Personal Growth Through Transformational Crises. Los Angeles: J. P. Tarcher.

Grof S. and Grof, C. 1989. Spiritual Emergency: When Personal Transformation Becomes a Crisis. Los Angeles: J. P. Tarcher.

Grof, S. 2009. "Holotropic Research and Archetypal Astrology." Archai: The Journal of Archetypal Cosmology, Vol. 1, Number 1.

Hillman, J. 2004. A Terrible Love of War. New York: Penguin.

Jung, C. G. 1950. "Psychology and National Problems." In: The Symbolic Life: Miscellaqneous Writings. Collected Works, vol. 918.

Bollingen Series XX, Princeton, N.J.: Princeton University Press.

Jung, C. G. 1959. The Archetypes and the Collective Unconscious. Collected Works, vol. 9,1. Bollingen Series XX, Princeton, N.J.: Princeton University Press.

Jung, C.G. 1960. "Synchronicity: An Acausal Connecting Principle." Collected Works, vol. 8, Bollingen Series XX. Princeton: Princeton UniversityPress.

Jung, C. G. 1964. "Wotan." In: Civilization in Transition. Collected Works, vol. 10. Bollingen Series XX, Princeton, N.J.: Princeton University Press.

Keen, S. 1988. Faces of the Enemy: Reflections of the Hostile Imagination. San Francisco: Harper.

Mause, L. de. 1975. The Independence of Psychohistory. In: The New Psychohistory. New York: The Psychohistory Press.

Plato 1961. Republic. In: The Collected Dialogues of Plato. Bollingen Series LXXI. Princeton, New Jersey: Princeton University Press.

Tarnas, R. 1993. The Passion of the Western Mind. New York: Harmony Books (Ballantine).
Tarnas, R. 2006. Cosmos and Psyche: Intimations of a New World View. New York: Viking Press

Bibliography

Campbell, Joseph, 1998, The Power of the Myth, Doubleday.

Campbell, Joseph, edited by Diane K. Osbon, 1991, Reflections on the Art of Living, Harper Collins.

Chomsky, 2003, Hegemony or Survival, The American Empire Project.

El Libro de los Libros de Chilam Balam, 2005, Fondo de Cultura Económica.

Epstein, Perle, 1978, Kabbakah, the Way of the Jewish Mystic, Shambala Clasics.

Grof, Stanislav, 2000, Psychology of the Future, Suny.

I Ching, El Libro de las Mutaciones, Eldhasa.

La Sagrada Biblia, Herder

Laszlo, Ervin, 2004, Science and the Akashic Field,Rochester Vermont.

Maciocia, Giovanni, 2005, The Foundations of Chinese Medicine, Elsevier.

Maitreya's Distinguishing Phenomena and Pure Being, commentary by Mipham.

Moriarty, John, 2006, Night Journey to Buddh Gaia, Lilliput.

Motoyama, Hiroshi, 2008, The Theories of the Chakras, New Age Books.

Müller-Ebeling, Claudia, Rätsch, Christian / Bahadur Shahi, Surendra, 2002, Shamanism and Tantra in the Himalayas, Inner Traditions.

Nietzsche, 1997, Untimely Meditations, Cambridge, Edited by Daniel Breazeale

Page Pliego, Jaime Tomás, el Mandato de los Dioses, UNAM.

Popol Vuh, Books.

Quinlan Forde, Ralph, 2008, The Book of Tibetan Medicine, Gaia.

Robinson, David, 1998, Neurobiology, Springer.

Santeria Cubana, Ediciones Nueva Vida.

Sun-Tzu, Penguin Books.

Swami Nityamuktananda Saraswati, 2005, Seeing Yoga, A

Contemplation of Patanjali's Yoga Sutras, Ediciones Ambrosía.

Swami Sadhanananda Giri, 1998, Kriya Yoga, Dr. Kalyan Bhattacharyea.

The Bhagavad Gita, commentary by Sri Aurobindo.

The Dhammapada, Rider.

The Kybalion and the Emerald Tablet.

The Principal Upanishads, Watkins.

The Tibetan Book of the Death, Penguin Books.

*'If I was alive today and all these year's wiser,
I would sing louder and harder than I ever did!'*
John Lennon

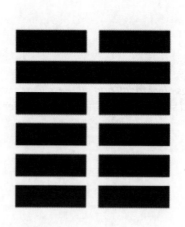